# THE THIRD MODE

## Towards a Green Society

# THE THIRD MODE

## Towards a Green Society

Jeff Olson

www.TheThirdMode.com

*The Third Mode: Towards a Green Society*
Copyright © 2012 by Jeff Olson
www.thethirdmode.com

ISBN: 978-0-9859335-1-7

# CONTENTS

# ACKNOWLEDGEMENTS

There are many people who have helped make this book possible. There are more of them than I can possibly thank or mention on these pages. You all know who you are, but here is a partial list of a few people and organizations who have helped me understand a new way of thinking.

Margo
Jaffa, Sarice and Izak
Alta Planning + Design
Barbara Glaser
Jim Kunstler
Bruce Piasceki, PhD
Harriet Fulbright
UAlbany
Lou Rossi
John Horsley
Sam Piper
The Grand Canyon Greenway Team

1

# PREFACE

When I first started working on green infrastructure, one of my mentors gave me some great advice. She said that every good presentation needs to have three basic parts: "What?", "So What?", and "Now What?" I've followed her advice, and it usually works. This book is organized around three sections: an introduction that defines the core topic ("What?"), ten chapters that make a series of key points linked to stories from projects that I have been involved in ("So What?"), and a conclusion that makes recommendations about how the lessons learned from these examples can be applied to future issues ("Now What?"). Throughout the book, I will return to a common theme: that there are more than two alternatives to solve any problem. That is why this book is called The Third Mode.

# *What?*

## INTRODUCTION
## The 10% Solution

I want you to think. I want you to read this book and think. I want you to read this book and think "this is a new way to solve problems." Every day, on a wide range of issues, we are required to find solutions. All too often, our thought process is limited to either-or decisions. We see this bi-modal pattern in politics (Republicans vs. Democrats), in business (profit and loss), in education (true or false) and in many other situations. I believe that this way of thinking limits our ability to solve major problems. I want you to think that there is another alternative, and it is called the third mode.

Several years ago, while I was working for the New York State Department of Transportation (NYSDOT) on the reauthorization of the federal transportation legislation known as ISTEA, I proposed that walking and bicycling be treated equally along with highways and mass transit. The reply I got from a senior policy bureaucrat was, "Are you crazy? – you're trying to create a third mode – and there are only two modes of transportation: highways and transit." It took me a while to realize that he was half right. I am trying to create a third mode – not just in terms of transportation, but in terms of the way we live, and in terms of the way we think.

Walking and bicycling are metaphors. While they are unique forms of mobility, they can also be thought of together to represent a "third mode" of transportation that is as important as highways and mass transit. This mode of transport, and the kind of thinking that is required to integrate it into our modern world, symbolizes a different perspective on our way of thinking. If you can understand why non-motorized mobility is important for transportation, you can also see how other problems could be resolved with similar thinking. Maybe our Republican vs. Democrat politics would benefit from a third political party. Maybe our health care system could be enhanced if people were more physically active in addition to being treated after they get sick. Maybe our energy policies could remove some of the demand for fossil fuels through conservation instead of drilling new oil wells.

Human powered transportation is often called an indicator species of urban environments. Like canaries in a coal mine, the presence of people walking and bicycling on our streets is a critical measure of a community's quality of life. Unfortunately, the significance of this critical mode of mobility is generally overshadowed by policies, plans and programs which focus only on motorized surface transportation: trains, trucks and automobiles. If we could think beyond defining transportation as simply highways and transit, we could move our society forward in both a physical and cultural sense.

In the late 1800s, Edward Abbott wrote a great book called "Flatland." Abbott was a mathematician who wanted to prove that there were more than three dimensions. His book describes a world that is flat, and its inhabitants are a hierarchical community of two dimensional shapes. The characters include a point, a line, a triangle, a square and a circle. The circle believes that it is the highest possible form of life because it has the maximum possible perimeter in their two dimensional world. Then, one day, the shapes are visited by a sphere – which passes through their world first as a point, then grows into circle before diminishing to a point again. The line, the triangle, the square and the circle can't even imagine that they have just seen something that is not only bigger than they are, but that it has a new dimension. By showing that a third dimension could not be recognized by the creatures of a two dimensional world, Abbott claimed to have proven that human beings would not be able to comprehend the existence of a fourth or greater dimension in our three dimensional world.

Abbott's Flatland is a parallel story to The Third Mode. By looking at non-motorized mobility as a third mode of transportation, I am trying to help you to think that multiple alternatives exist to solve many problems that are currently defined by two opposites. The solutions are often right in front of us, if we choose to think in the third mode. This requires having a big picture perspective that allows us to see multiple possibilities. Just as Abbott demonstrated in the 1800's that it may be possible to imagine more than three dimensions, third mode thinking provides the opportunity to apply new solutions to contemporary challenges. My emphasis is on sustainable, active, healthy transportation because it's the field I've spent a lot of my life working in, and also because it illustrates the potential for a new way of solving problems in general.

For years, the U.S. treated non-motorized transportation as if it did not even exist. Every decade, the U.S. Census provided detailed statistics for highway and transit modes, but there was often one section of every transportation data pie chart that simply said "other." When my boss at NYSDOT, Louis Rossi, the Director of the Planning Division, asked his data experts to show what "other" meant, it turned out that it showed more than 7% of commuter travel in New York State was being done by pedestrians and bicyclists. For non-commuter travel, the number jumped to more than 20% of all trips. This was shocking news to the status quo – for the first time, we had data that showed more people walked and bicycled to work in upstate NY than were using public transportation, carpooling or any other mode of travel except driving a car.

Nobody at NYSDOT had figured out what was hidden behind that data, and the reality of what it meant for the third mode to have such a significant role in transportation planning. At that time, New York State was investing billions of dollars on highways and transit projects, but next to nothing was being spent on a very significant mode of transportation. As the State's Bicycle and Pedestrian Program Manager, I used that data to nickname my office "The Department of Other." We posted a simple pair of signs in the planning conference room with the words 'bicycle' and 'pedestrian' on them, just to be sure that the third mode would literally be in the room for every meeting.

For many years, the "Department of Other," and groups like it throughout the U.S., have faced an uphill battle. Underlying the conventional wisdom on American transportation is a cultural bias that has developed along with our modern fossil-fueled society. We are a suburban, sprawling, fast food nation. At the time of the 2000 presidential elections in the U.S., the American population had become 50% suburban. This is a serious piece of information – it represents the first time in human history that a nation has gone from agricultural to urban and then back to something halfway in between. Second and third generation suburban citizens are now growing up in a built environment better suited for automobiles than for people. Our land use, taxation, economic and social systems are all connected to these underlying facts of our built environment.

In most of the U.S., if you are not old enough to drive, if you don't have a car, or if you are too old to drive, you are trapped living in a place where it often takes a gallon of gas to go get a gallon of milk. And the gallon of gas is cheaper. Even worse, we've created a world where it makes some kind of twisted economic sense to drive a huge SUV a short distance to a store to buy a bottle of water that was imported from Fiji. That water had to be bottled from a spring on an island in the Pacific, shipped halfway around the world, refrigerated in a store, and sold by a person at the counter – and that water somehow costs less than the fuel in the SUV. At some point, we have to see examples like this as further evidence that there is something really wrong with our long term view of the global economy.

In spite of two decades of U.S. transportation policy that has at least allowed non-motorized transport to be an eligible use of federal funding, most American communities still look as if the term "transportation" is synonymous with "requiring the use of fossil fuels." In many places, there is still a giggle factor when walking and bicycling are proposed as a solution for sustainable mobility, energy conservation, air quality improvements, economic development, improved health and fitness, or other important issues. Rational arguments have been well supported for all of these common goods, and yet the third mode is rarely given a chance to be a major part of the solution to these bigger issues.

The root of our conventional wisdom is an underlying Western need to split any problem into opposing sides. We think that transportation must be solved by providing either more highways or mass transit. Environmentalists are defined as being anti-development. Economic issues are a debate between rich and poor. As a result, complex issues such as climate change cannot even be discussed because there are so many causes and effects, so many issues that cannot be defined as black and white, yes or no, good or bad. The end result is often crisis-driven policies. We are unable to be proactive because our two dimensional thinking is destined to create narrow, sound-bite driven frameworks in which to solve our problems. We need a new third mode of thinking as much as we need a third mode of transportation.

Just to be clear, it is important to make the point that the solutions proposed in these pages are, at best, partial solutions. I have often said that walking and bicycling could optimistically represent 10% of U.S. transportation. But even if this were all that we can accomplish, bear in mind that it could be done with just a fraction of our nation's infrastructure funding. For decades, more than 90% of federal transportation funding has been spent to build our current mono-modal system. Let's be generous and say that 5% of U.S. federal transportation spending went to the third mode, and we did achieve the goal of moving 10% of all trips with that amount funding. That would be a return that any investor would be happy with in our current economy.

The economics of this kind of solution are real. For example, the City of Portland, Oregon, has developed enough bikeway infrastructure over the past decade to achieve between 5 and 10 percent of the city's urban trips by bicycle – at a cost of less than building one mile of urban highway. This return on investment is significant because it not only improves transportation, but also because it provides significant health, environmental, economic and quality of life benefits. Portland's efforts have also led to a new bicycle economy based on manufacturing, construction, retail, tourism and related new businesses. More than a billion dollars a year are recirculated in the Portland region due to these investments. The city has a long way to go before it matches the success of global leaders like Amsterdam and Copenhagen (where more than 30% of travel is done by bicycle), but Portland has created living proof that the third mode can work, even in America.

In a more specific example, cities throughout the U.S. have added bike racks to their public bus systems. This simple improvement has resulted in increases in transit ridership at a fraction of the cost of conventional transit projects such as building new rail lines or transit stations. By combining bicycling and transit, the service area is significantly increased at transit stops, since people can quickly bike farther and faster than they can walk to the bus. It took a lot of effort to convince transit agencies that they would increase ridership by making improvements for another mode of travel. This is a prime example of third mode thinking. The bike racks on buses have shown a positive return on investment for the transit agencies that installed them. That return is a rare accomplishment in the transportation field, because traditional highway and transit infrastructure investments often require huge costs to achieve similar benefits.

In terms of health care, the U.S. and other nations are spending significant resources on treating the effects of a global physical inactivity epidemic that is caused by a combination of poor diets, lack of exercise and genetics. Over the past decade, the health community has taken an increasingly pro-active role in making the connection between the built environment, walkable communities and improved public health outcomes. However, this has not occurred without a significant effort by walking and bicycling advocates to convince health leaders that such simple solutions can have such wide ranging benefits. A decade ago, many hospitals, health agencies, drug makers and policy makers assumed that the key to solving the obesity crisis was the 'magic pill' of new drugs, diets and encouraging people to vaguely 'get more exercise.' Now, research is showing a strong connection between human health and community design. Building sidewalks, striping bike lanes and promoting active transportation are third mode solutions that are reducing the cost of health care. Instead of treating patients after they get sick from a lack of physical activity, these solutions combine redesigning our built environment to be more walkable with traditional medical interventions.

The environmental benefits of walking and bicycling would probably seem like an obvious source of common ground for advocates and leaders in the sustainable mobility and green movements to support. Unfortunately, this is yet another area where 'either-or' kinds of thinking have limited potentially powerful collaborations. Mainstream environmental organizations have dealt with big issues like climate change by focusing on solutions such as carbon trading systems, new government regulations and political advocacy. There is generally less effort being spent to encourage simpler solutions such as energy conservation, recycling or non-motorized transportation. This approach is typified in Al Gore's film "Earth in the Balance." The former Vice President is a hero for making a compelling case about climate change at the 50,000 foot level. But, the only forms of transportation he personally uses in the movie are airplanes and limousines. It isn't until the credits are rolling that "Earth in the Balance" suggests any specific actions that an individual can do to be part of the solution. This is a missed opportunity. While leaders like Al Gore discuss big-picture, long-term options like carbon taxes and cap-and-trade systems, years are going by in which simple third mode solutions are not being acted upon.

Another example of the gap between the green and active mobility movements is the environmental approval process required to get an infrastructure project built in the U.S. On federally funded projects, the process falls under the National Environmental Policy Act (NEPA), a law created during the era of big polluters and projects that rammed highways and garbage incinerators through in urban neighborhoods. To get a project approved under NEPA, you are required to receive a "Finding of No Significant Impact" (yes, the acronym is "FONSI"), based on a detailed analysis of environmental concerns such as wetlands, cultural/historic resources, and other factors. If you are building a sidewalk, a bicycle lane, a trail, or other infrastructure that is good for both people and the environment, there is no process under NEPA that determines if you have a "Finding of Positive Environmental Benefit." As a result, bike, pedestrian and trail projects throughout the U.S. are frequently delayed and incur significant costs because they are being treated by regulations that did not imagine a positive solution as a potential outcome.

The same issue is true in many states. In New York, the State Environmental Quality Review Act (SEQRA) requires that a project receive a "Negative Declaration" to prove that it has no adverse environmental impacts. There is no process under SEQRA for giving projects a "Positive Declaration of Environmental Benefits." Taken to an extreme, this inability to see certain types of infrastructure projects as being good for the environment is being used in unintended ways. In San Francisco, the Transportation Department was sued for developing the city's innovative network of bike lanes without submitting a full environmental impact statement. The bike network program was significantly delayed for several years while the lawsuit was being resolved.

This isn't how we should be thinking if we are trying to quickly implement the kind of green, sustainable solutions that will solve major environmental problems. It is a constant challenge to get leaders to believe that third mode solutions such as bike, pedestrian and trail infrastructure projects are of significant value. In the U.S., traditional big-ticket development projects are often based on the model of subsidized infrastructure for highways and transit, combined with land use and taxation policies that support conventional economic growth based on cheap fossil fuels. "Smart Growth" codes and policies are moving forward in many states and communities, but they are not the mainstream.

In his landmark book, "Small Is Beautiful: *Economics As If People Mattered,*" British economist E. F. Schumacher made a strong case for investment in least cost, sustainable solutions. He argued convincingly that it is simple technologies that individuals can understand and control that will have the greatest benefit and require our biggest investment. If we followed his lead as a society, we would be looking for simple, real solutions that work to solve problems with the least energy and cost. Instead, modern society continues to look to the next big ticket technological fix for our economic success. This is not sustainable.

Whether the reason is economics, environment, health or mobility, the bottom line continues to be how we approach these types of issues and how we choose to develop solutions. In his book "The Unschooled Mind: *How Children Think and How Schools Should Teach*," Howard Gardner presents a clear case for moving beyond either-or, black-or white, yes-or-no modes of thinking. Gardner's concepts provide a foundation for seeing third mode solutions for our infrastructure, and also as a way of finding solutions for larger problems. To use transportation as a metaphor, if all we are trying to solve is the problem of providing highways and transit systems, we will never do more than provide partial solutions for mobility. Like a bumper sticker from the 1970's once said, "the greatest danger of our age is total obsession with partial ideas." If, instead, we start solving problems by looking beyond just two opposite alternatives, then we have a chance to create real solutions that will work.

I've been involved in a lot of projects over the last 25 years. I think that the stories on these pages are important because they are symbolic of larger trends that are happening globally and acted out locally. My career has taken me from the private sector as an architect, to co-founding a non-profit smart growth planning organization, to a role in the public sector at the New York State Department of Transportation, to serving as director of the White House Millennium Trails Program, and then back to the private sector as a partner with an internationally recognized consulting firm, Alta Planning + Design.

I have been fortunate to be involved in projects that have included urban greenways systems, complete streets, safe routes to school, National Parks, private properties, corporate clients and projects in Canada, Mexico, and the United Arab Emirates. I have also served on the faculty of the State University of New York at Albany for 15 years and have guest lectured at schools including Cornell, BOKU Vienna, the University of Virginia, and others. I have worked as a community volunteer on a variety of projects and served on committees and advisory boards of national organizations including the Transportation Research Board, Mississippi River Trail and East Coast Greenway. The common thread in all of this work has been to work towards making the world more sustainable by using third mode solutions, one project at a time.

There was a time when I was one of a handful of people who believed that transportation solutions based on walking, bicycling and trails were an essential part of global sustainability. Today, this issue is part of rapidly growing international movement. A while ago, Dan Burden of Walkable Communities, Inc. told me, "We'll always have work to do, because every street is a project." Dan is truly the Johnny Appleseed of our profession and has travelled to hundreds of communities, so his advice has always stayed with me. What is so interesting now is that a shift is taking place and these ideas are gaining traction at much higher levels.

On June 4, 2010, Bloomberg News ran a story titled, *"Mayors Beat World Leaders Promoting Cycle Paths,"* describing how global cities are taking the lead on sustainable mobility, even as repeated attempts at large scale multinational climate change treaties continue to be delayed. Similar initiatives are happening around the world, and the challenge is to be able to capitalize on opportunities in a variety of cultures. While New York, Mexico City and Paris move forward with new bikeways, Shanghai made a recent attempt to eliminate its famous bicycling streets. In many places in China, India and the developing nations of the world, the bicycle is still perceived as transportation for poor people who can't afford a car. Walking is often considered even less important, and all over the world pedestrians are forced to walk along and across roadways that were designed as if people didn't exist.

While it is frequently said in public debates that this is happening because of a lack of funding, that is hard to accept in nations where billions of dollars are spent on public works projects. The problem isn't having the funds, it's about the choices we make in how we spend the money. According to the USDOT's Highway Traffic Noise website, through the end of 2004, more than 2,200 linear miles of highway noise barrier walls had been built in the U.S. at a cost of over $3.4 billion (in 2004 dollars). That cost dwarfs the amount of U.S. spending on projects for walking and bicycling during the same period. If the U.S. wanted to build more sidewalks, safe crossings, bikeways, complete streets and trails, that amount of funding would go a long way to making the third mode into a mainstream solution. Unfortunately, the decisions that are made to fund the ever growing costs of the motor-vehicle industrial complex simply do not see the value in "other" modes of transportation.

If aliens landed on our planet, there is a good chance that they would think the motor vehicles were the intelligent life forms and that people were their servants. If you look at a satellite photo of most American cities, the highways look like the veins and arteries of some mythical beast. The automobile and all of its infrastructure have become powerful symbols of modern society. Road safety, especially for vulnerable road users (a euphemism for pedestrians and bicyclists) has become an epidemic on wheels. In June, 2007, the Pope issued a "*Drivers' Ten Commandments*" that included "IX". On the road, protect the more vulnerable party." If this global problem is so big that the Pope has to weigh in on it, then the time has come to find some real solutions.

The 2010 Bloomberg story about the world's mayors said that Los Angeles plans to spend $230 million on 1,700 miles of bicycle facilities, and Copenhagen will spend $1.6 billion by 2012 on bike paths, green energy projects, and retrofitting city buildings, Melbourne plans to ban cars from its downtown and offer incentives to developers who invest in efficiency. London is opening designated cycling lanes across the capital in an effort to add 120,000 cycle trips per day and the City has made 6,000 bikes available for the public to rent. "It's a green gold rush," Melbourne Lord Mayor Robert Doyle said in an interview. London's Mayor Boris Johnson considered car-free days to fight pollution, and rode with 65,000 cyclists across London to highlight his programs. Washington DC, New York City and Boston have all been transformed into recipients of "silver" level Bicycle Friendly Communities awards from the League of American Bicyclists, and all three cities are implementing public bike sharing systems.

These are extraordinary changes, and they are now happening at an increasing pace thanks to community leaders around the world who have realized that walking and bicycling are real solutions that move cities forward. In forward moving cities, third mode thinking is a common element of change. Leaders are realizing that now is the time for new ways to think that lead to new ways to solve problems. The difference between third mode solutions for mobility and many of the other previous approaches to solving big picture issues is the ability to create real solutions that work. These are not futuristic visions that depend on some new technology. These solutions are not based on the words of issue entrepreneurs who simply capitalize on public fears of problems they cannot control. The third mode is a model for how mobility can work, and mobility provides a model of how we can apply this kind of thinking to a wide range of other issues.

The following chapters will take a closer look at these issues through the lens of real projects and case studies at a range of scales, from local efforts to national initiatives. Since transportation infrastructure is one of the fundamental elements of the built environment, sustainable mobility is an integral issue at the local, state, national and global levels. The common thread is that walking and bicycling are a metaphor for a third mode way of looking at and finding solutions to a wide range of problems. In a world of shrinking resources, limited public and private sector budgets, global competition and a perception that the issues we face are too big for individuals and organizations to change, now is the time to realize the value of thinking in new ways. This is an appropriate point to start thinking in the third mode. As Einstein said, the solution to a problem cannot come from within the system that created it.

# *So What?*

## 1. HIGHWAYS VS TRANSIT

## A Classic Paradox

If you live in a place where walking and bicycling have been left out of the built environment, you may wonder, "Why is this place built just for cars?" Even a child can look at a typical street and see that there needs to be a safe place to walk or ride a bicycle. Yet, over the past fifty years, cities around the world have been built without the infrastructure for these basic forms of mobility. This is because community leaders, elected officials, and public works agencies have been focused for decades on moving things with motors, and not on creating places for people. The things with motors include planes, trains, trucks, buses and automobiles. Vast amounts of wealth have been poured into creating a very sophisticated infrastructure to move these motor vehicles though, around and between places. Unfortunately, not enough effort has been spent moving people within these places.

In many U.S. communities, it is common to see streets with missing sidewalks, bus stops that consist of no more than a small sign stuck in the dirt on the side of the road, intersections that are impossible to safely walk cross, and with a complete lack of infrastructure for bicycling. Fixing these problems is not rocket science. It takes an eye for detail and an understanding that small scale solutions can help solve bigger problems. It is hard to believe that the same nation that sent astronauts to the moon can't make it safe for people to walk across the street. As a friend of mine used to say, "You have to make the easy ones look difficult so the hard ones look impossible." Our current infrastructure proves this point.

Often, in their efforts to overcome these issues, American engineers will build sidewalks into their road projects, and claim "now we've done what is needed for pedestrians and bicyclists." Since bicyclists (with the exception of children and seniors) legally have the right to ride on the road, this often makes the problem worse. Because these engineers assume that pedestrians and bicyclists are the same thing, they have failed to accommodate bicyclists on the road, and have then forced the bicyclists to ride on the sidewalk, which is often against the law and makes the sidewalk unsafe for pedestrians.

The issue isn't that these well-intentioned engineers aren't trying to solve the problem. It's that they are only solving one isolated part of the problem. In the transition from designing streets primarily for automobiles towards a more third mode approach, the designers of these projects have at least recognized that there are, in fact, other people using the road. They just haven't figured out who these people are and how best to design for them. It's a big leap to include pedestrian facilities into projects that didn't have them before. However, at a basic level, pedestrians belong on the sidewalk and bicyclists belong on the road. Understanding that simple fact of infrastructure will be a major step forward as communities try to evolve beyond the monoculture of motorized traffic.

Once we reach the point of understanding that pedestrians, bicyclists, cars, trucks, buses, trains and other forms of transportation are part of an interconnected system, it is then possible to see how finely grained these issues can be. For example, "pedestrians" is a very broad term that includes transit customers, people who walk for fitness, families who enjoy tourism, kids who bike to school, seniors who are slower to cross the street, and people with disabilities such as vision, hearing and physical challenges. Bicyclists are another diverse group, including high- speed road bicyclists, urban bike commuters, children, seniors, touring bicyclists, mountain bikers and others. Motorized forms of travel have similar distinctions, including commuters, tourists, truckers, bus drivers and others. In fact, a majority of the trips made on the U.S. roads aren't made by people commuting to work.

I personally fit into many of these descriptions, and can be several of these types of travelers in the same day. I might walk my child to school in the morning, bike to the bank during the day, and go on a fast road bike ride that afternoon with friends. I could just as easily go out for a walk with my wife in the evening, take a bus across town, and drive to the airport or train station the next day. You may find it ironic that I teach a course on walking and bicycling at a university that is 30 miles away from my home, and that I have to drive to the campus. I don't see this as a big deal, because I often combine my trips to the university with other meetings, and since on most days I don't have to drive a car at all.

My point is that there are a wide variety of trips that people make for both transportation and recreation. There really aren't separate groups of people who can be pigeon-holed as 'pedestrians' or 'bicyclists' or 'transit riders' or 'motorists.' We all travel in different ways at different times of day, at different times of our lives, and to different destinations. I'm not trying to be a purist. We don't all have to suddenly give up our cars. We only need to walk or bike ten percent of the time to make a significant change in society. That is just two days of walking, bicycling or taking transit per month for a typical commuter. We can meet this goal, but first we have to overcome the fact that too many people have become dependent on their cars as the only form of mobility, and that our communities have been designed only for that single mode of transportation.

At a macro scale, our petroleum addiction has become ingrained in policy at the local, state and national levels. When it comes to infrastructure policy for motorists, we don't distinguish between a trip to work and a trip for fun. We build roads for people to drive to beaches, ski resorts and other 'non-essential' destinations. But, when it comes time to fund a pedestrian or bicyclist facility, it is common to hear that it is a "recreation" project and is therefore less important than infrastructure for motorists. The argument between "transportation" and "recreation" is just another example of bi-modal thinking. Especially as technology changes the global workplace, more people are able to choose where they want to live, work and play. The places that can combine transportation and recreation have a significant advantage in creating the quality of life required for the economy of the next generation.

Most of the public debate surrounding transportation in the U.S. has been focused on funding for "highways" (i.e. facilities for cars and trucks) and "transit" (i.e. buses and trains) as if they were separate, and often competing, modes of travel. Clearly, transportation is not so simple - a bus runs on a highway, people walk on streets after parking their cars, and there are many combinations of trips and purposes. For example, a bicyclist riding on a street with bike lanes to get to the bus stop and then using a bike rack on a bus is both a "highway" and a "transit" customer. The reality is that highways and transit are parts of an integrated transportation system - and that those two parts of the system are connected by the third mode: walking and bicycling. Although this may seem obvious, it represents a major paradigm shift with significant implications for transportation agencies and the traveling public.

While pundits argue between funding for "highways" and "transit," all this does is create a back-and-forth debate and no forward motion. Don't get me wrong, I am a supporter of both transit and highways – as long as they are used as a balanced parts of holistic mobility solutions. It's hard to imagine the world's great cities without their transit systems – Tokyo, London, Singapore, New York, Toronto and many others are good examples. It's equally hard to imagine Germany without the Autobahn or the U.S. without the interstate highways. At the same time, planners often assume that the only way to create successful mobility is to either build mass transit or new highways. Since there are more than two modes of travel, the real challenge that communities face is how to 'right-size' their infrastructure investments so that they are sustainable.

What if we imagined a more integrated "third mode" future? Someday, our interstate highways may be automated, with private vehicles operated on web-based autopilot networks between major cities. Existing cities, re-developed suburban town centers, and new towns (based on recent New Urbanist communities such as Celebration, Florida) will be designed around pedestrians, with bicycles and private cars providing personal mobility. Rapid bus systems operated by the private sector will be able to serve smart growth development patterns by simply providing routes which connect town centers. Trails and greenways will be an integrated component of community design, and every street will have bike lanes, sidewalks and safe pedestrian crossings. Children will safely walk and bike to school. High speed rail will link major urban centers, and air travel will be focused to connect longer distances. The web will link businesses between communities without physical travel. Sounds like a great place to live, doesn't it?

This vision is hard to imagine within the constraints of the current American battle between highways and transit. Creating livable communities requires an integrated approach that goes far beyond the current debate. Our federal and state transportation programs were developed for the interstate era, and trying to build anything else is like shooting an elephant with an ant gun. The U.S. provides a small amount of federal aid to transportation 'enhancements' for non-motorized travel, but we don't have an integrated program that provides equally for all modes of travel. This is because of our bias towards the automobile, our bi-polar system of thinking about transportation as only "highways" and "transit," and our inability to see that the sustainable solution requires a third mode approach to the problem.

If we could design all roads as multi-use facilities for cars, trucks, buses, pedestrians and bicyclists, we would be able to move our society with greater efficiency. We would stop building arterial highways that serve as barriers between neighborhoods. We would realize that while fixed rail transit is a great idea for areas with the right mix of urban density and land use policy, mass transit is not the only option for creating great communities. We would understand that not every town needs a huge highway bypass – and in fact these projects often kill the downtowns they are trying to save. If we could develop smart growth town centers around pedestrian and bicyclist mobility, we could achieve livability – and then we could use highways and transit to connect these centers to other destinations. If we built in this pattern and re-focused our infrastructure investments on a balanced solution for all modes of travel, we might even have enough funding to pay for it.

If we don't make this change, it is also possible that our future will not be so optimistic. It is unlikely that our society will be able to continue to support a fossil-fueled, motorized infrastructure into the next generation. The financial, taxation and land use systems that support individual car and suburban home ownership are not sustainable. We may find that we are forced by crisis to shift to more cost effective forms of travel such as walking and bicycling. We may end up in a fractured nation of regions like Ernest Callenbach's novel "Ecotopia," where the Northwest secedes from the U.S. to create its own sustainable country. There are plenty of doomsday scenarios out there, with economic collapse and a return to a much more basic existence. I choose to believe that there is a positive way forward if we can think in new ways.

When you think beyond the highways vs. transit debate, its inherent paradoxes are revealed. Big highway projects are linked to big contracts, and the companies that benefit from these contracts wield considerable political power. The same is true for public transit funding, which in the U.S., is in turn linked to unionized labor organizations that lobby for public transit funding. The "other" modes of bicycling and walking do not have the same organized power to influence significant city, state and national funding. They are therefore limited to projects that are much smaller by comparison, and often have to rely on volunteer-based non-profit organizations for advocacy. While, in the U.S., highway and transit agencies are represented on the policy boards of most Metropolitan Planning Organizations (MPOS's), there is no voting interest for walking and bicycling in these key agencies. This political power imbalance relates directly to the inability to get beyond the highway vs. transit paradox.

Vested interests are hard to change, and even the most successful bicyclist and pedestrian advocacy efforts are dwarfed by the scale and resources of the highway and transit lobbies. In a two-party political system that is fighting a battle between two alternatives, it will take either enlightened leadership or a major crisis for change to happen. If gas prices in the U.S. begin to match the prices around the world – and if that price increase is captured in public sector infrastructure revenues - then that could be the catalyst for leveling the playing field for sustainable transportation. Conversely, if enough of our elected leaders realize that walking and bicycling facilities are 'must have" features of their communities, then political change can result in new solutions. In the meantime, walking and bicycling advocates are trapped between the bigger modes and struggling to be part of the big picture.

I remember meeting with a group of bicyclists who were riding across the country. One of the riders was wearing a t-shirt that said, "Coalition for an Asphalt Moratorium." When we asked what the group had ridden their bikes across the country on, they said, "roads." It seemed bizarre that they would be campaigning against asphalt while riding 3,000 miles on roads paved with asphalt. I know what they meant – they were tired of seeing huge roads built without provisions for pedestrians and bicyclists. By defining their mission in oppositional terms, they were actually opposing the solution they desired. The idea of a "better roads" movement would have been a more appropriate way to get more asphalt designed in better ways for pedestrians, bicyclists, transit customers and motorists. Since there is currently no third mode consensus that all of these interests are part of a common system, we are unable to gather broad public support for infrastructure funding and programs.

There was a time in U.S. history when this was not the case. In the late 1800s, America experienced a surge in new mobility when the modern bicycle was first made popular. The original League of American Wheelmen (L.A.W.), now the League of American Bicyclists (L.A.B.), had more than 100,000 members and led what was called the Good Roads Movement in the 1890's. It was early bicycling advocates who lobbied for the first paved roads to be built in the U.S. The bicycling movement was part of a major social change that included the liberation of women, who gained the right to vote at the same time that the bicycle gave them an independent means to travel without a chaperone. Today, women on bikes are one of the key indicators of successful cities, in part because women are more likely to ride if good, safe, bikeway facilities are provided.

In a strange twist of fate, the early L.A.W. split off a group that became the American Automobile Association (AAA). Although the two groups once shared a common heritage of safer roads, they are now often seen as political enemies. In contemporary transportation politics, bicycling and walking advocates are generally assumed to be allies of the environmental and mass transit sectors. Their common enemy is supposedly the "highway lobby." The highway lobby is made up of the people who build roads and bridges. The highway people are assumed to perceive the transit, walking and bicycling people as their enemies. Unfortunately, the transit people are primarily concerned with running their buses and trains, and have rarely supported spending "their" funding on pedestrians and bicyclists, who are their customers.

In 2002, the League of American Bicyclists started hosting an annual Bike Summit in Washington, D.C. I was asked to help moderate one of the first summit panels. My idea for the session was to invite the highway lobby to the table. I asked the powerful American Association of State Highway and Transportation Officials (AASHTO) to sponsor a panel to talk about how bicycling advocates could work with the "highway lobby" to be part of a modern Better Roads Movement. There were plenty of hard core bike advocates in the room who were opposed to having AASHTO on the program, and they made their voices heard. At the same time, the idea of collaboration was at least discussed, and clearly the opportunity was created to share common ground. By 2009, AASHTO was invited to share the podium at the Bike Summit, along with the American Public Transit Association (APTA), in a rare moment of third mode advocacy.

Unfortunately, the challenges of the current economy and the ingrained nature of the highways vs. transit paradox continue to limit the ability for multiple modes to reach common ground. As recently as the spring of 2011, AASHTO's member states developed a resolution to oppose the inclusion of funding for walking and bicycling in the next round of federal transportation funding. That measure was tabled, but if they keep putting ideas like that forward, it's no wonder the bicycling advocates don't like working with the highway lobby. It seems like we're stuck in a loop. State Departments of Transportation continue to emphasize highway and bridge projects as their primary mission, and transit agencies continue to focus their resources on operating buses and trains. Since funding is limited, this narrow, one-mode-at-a-time perspective continues to leave bicycling and walking out from a wide variety of key projects and programs.

Ultimately, there are really no 'sides' in the highways vs. transit paradox. It will take collaboration between all modes of travel to get us out of these back-and-forth debates. We need to realize, as a society, that every trip begins as a pedestrian, even if you just walk to your garage and get in the car, or walk down the street to use public transportation. U.S. federal transportation policy needs a reset, and that change has to come from a new vision of sustainable mobility as the core infrastructure to create livable communities. Without this kind of change, we are destined to keep making decisions that maintain the highways vs. transit paradox and leave the third mode out of the solution.

Every time I am at Grand Central Station in New York, I am reminded of these issues. In the late 1990s, a new source of funding called Transit Enhancements was made available through the Federal Transit Administration (FTA). This program paralleled the much larger Transportation Enhancements funding that was available through the Federal Highway Administration (FWHA). The transit enhancements legislation included eligibility for a wide range of potential projects, including bicyclist and pedestrian facilities, historic preservation projects and transportation museums.

New York City, because of its extensive public transit system, was the largest recipient of transit enhancements funds in the country. Progressive mobility advocates suggested that new bike parking and pedestrian crossings be installed at the City's transit stops with that funding. Instead, the majority of the money ended up being used to restore the mural of the constellations on the ceiling in Grand Central Station's Great Hall. I'm not saying that restoring an historic transportation landmark isn't a good idea. It's just that if we have limited transportation money to spend, our highest priority should be moving people. Because it was perceived as "transit" funding, the pedestrian and bicyclist improvements were not seen as important in the transit enhancements funding process.

While bicycling and pedestrian advocates continue to assume that they are on the same side as the transit agencies, and that highways are the enemy, it is still unlikely that transit or highway agencies will spend funding allocated to them on other modes of transportation. After decades of these kinds of decisions, new solutions are slowly being put in place, but they are mainly exceptions to business as usual. Recently, a new Federal Transit Administration policy has been approved that allows transit funding to be used for pedestrian and bicyclist improvements within the area around transit stops and stations. Innovative projects, including a new Washington, DC Bike Station and the Boston Bike Share system are now being implemented using federal transit funding. Still, America lags far behind other parts of the world in creating integrated third mode infrastructure solutions.

If you sent a typical American to visit the Netherlands or Denmark, they would come back with pictures of bicyclists and pedestrians. In Amsterdam, Copenhagen and other cities, the levels of bicycle use exceed 30% of all transportation. Bicycles are everywhere, and have been made a routine part of daily life. Pedestrian priority streets are key parts of the urban fabric. A large percentage of the bicyclists are women, children and seniors – because the facilities are safe. This is an extraordinary accomplishment in today's world. The Dutch and Danes are not satisfied with these levels, and are pushing to reach 50% of all urban trips being done by bicycle. This is happening in modern, technologically advanced, successful nations. Cities in Germany, Spain, France, England, and other nations are achieving similar successes. Advocates, political and business leaders are fighting against the conventional wisdom of modern fossil fuel-based society. They are winning because they integrate all modes of transport in their systems of urban planning and development.

It is particularly interesting that, in the Netherlands and Denmark, most of their great bicycle and pedestrian infrastructure was built after World War II – at the same time that America's suburban sprawl was developed. The incredible people-friendly streets of Amsterdam and Copenhagen have not always been there. They were intentionally created in response to societal issues of energy, health, economy and community. This was accomplished in a post-war crisis environment, where there were critical needs to rebuild bombed-out cities, to deal with food and fuel shortages, and to rebuild national economies. These conditions are, in many ways, very similar to the issues we face in the world today.

There is no single solution for every community, but common themes are emerging to create integrated mobility solutions in innovative cities around the world. Metropolises including Bogota, Seoul, New Delhi and Mexico City are developing new urban corridors based on Bus Rapid Transit (BRT) systems. They are creating great streets for bicycling, walking and transit – without the cost of building fixed rail systems. The buses run on asphalt streets, but have stations designed to look and operate like high-tech modern rail stations. People can easily walk and bike to the bus, and the buses are more flexible to operate than trains. This kind of innovation changes the highways vs. transit paradox into a new, integrated way of creating urban mobility. Most of the innovation in new BRT systems is happening in developing nations and not in the U.S., in large part due to the ingrained nature of our highways vs. transit thinking.

Another example of how innovative mobility is prevented by treating highways transit and the third mode separately is the jitney vans that are common in communities throughout Latin America and the Caribbean. Jitneys are operated privately, and the price and supply of vans matches the demand of ridership. They operate on public streets, and people generally walk to and from jitney stops that are along popular routes for short trips across and between towns. This solution would seem to fit the entrepreneurial model of the American Dream: a private operator invests in a vehicle, maintains it for the customers, finds a market for services, and makes money serving that market.

Unfortunately, in the U.S., these kinds of systems have faced aggressive reactions from the existing transportation industry. Publicly funded mass transit agencies have fought to crack down on privately run jitneys, which are seen as competing with "their" fixed route bus services. The arguments include the fact that jitneys cost less because they are not operated by unionized labor, they do not have to meet insurance and licensing regulations, and they 'steal' riders from publicly regulated bus routes. Similar challenges have been faced by pedal taxis, car sharing systems and other innovative new privately run services that are trying to find their niche within the existing highway and transit systems. At the same time, a combination of BRT systems, privately run jitneys, pedal taxis, walking and bicycling could be cost-effectively operated on existing roads in many American communities – if we can find our way out of the highways vs. transit paradox.

In the U.S., it is important to remember that the urban transit systems in cities like Boston, New York, and Chicago, along with most of our national rail infrastructure, was originally built by the private sector. After the construction of publicly funded highway systems around and through many American cities, it became necessary to form public authorities to continue operating the mass transit systems due to increased competition from the automobile. The resulting bureaucracy created new publicly funded agencies with parallel (and often competing) agendas that reinforce the highways vs. transit paradox. These agencies often treat highways, transit, walking and bicycling as unrelated topics.

That is why, for example, the Metropolitan Transit Authority (MTA) in New York produced a 1994 plan for the City's bus service that was called *"Faster Than Walking: Street Congestion and New York City Transit."* Walking and transit should have been seen as integrated elements of that plan, not as competing opposites. At that time, the City's streets were functioning at an average speed of less than ten miles per hour – an ideal speed for pedestrians and bicyclists. Focusing on making the buses run faster than people could walk was a mono-modal way to frame the problem.

On the "highway" side, the State Departments of Transportation continue to argue that there is not enough money to maintain and expand our existing road systems. Every year, the interstate highways get older and require more money for maintenance and operations. These costs include road and bridge repairs, snow plowing, emergency response, law enforcement and the hidden costs of pollution and health related impacts. We can't continue to fund this system forever. The federal gas tax in the U.S. is still fixed at less than twenty cents per gallon. We need to add three letters to the legislation and change this to a twenty "per" cent tax – then as the price goes up over time, we will generate the revenue to change our infrastructure. That is the kind of thinking that can shift the funding battle between highways and transit into a third mode solution.

In the U.S., the playing field is not level between highways, transit and non-motorized travel, in part because only highways and transit have a seat at the table. If you look at a funding pie chart for New York State, roughly half of the available transportation funds are allocated to mass transit, and the other half goes to highways. Walking and bicycling only receive a small fraction of the funding – if you cut the pie chart with a knife, walking and bicycling would be the crumbs on the knife after the pie was sliced in half. This happens in spite of the fact that walking and bicycling provide more than seven percent of commuter travel in New York State, and pedestrians and bicyclists represent more than 25 percent of traffic fatalities.

We should be allocating funding based on two simple pie charts: the percentage of existing travel for each mode of transportation, and the future mode share that we are trying to achieve. If we want to have ten percent of all trips accomplished by walking and bicycling, then at some point our investment needs to match that goal. We've become so used to debating the issue in terms of "highways vs. transit," we fail to notice that a broader perspective is a key to solving the problem. Until our local, state and national leaders are convinced that transportation requires a fully multi-modal vision, it is hard to imagine generating support for the funding needed to create the infrastructure of a 21st century nation.

Regardless of the type of transportation systems we build, every community has the opportunity to re-think its priorities based on a 'third mode' perspective. A great example of this was shown when the TV series the Simpsons featured an episode called *"Marge vs. the Monorail."* In a classic parody of

transportation in America, a slick salesman tries to convince
Springfield that a new monorail is the solution to all of the
city's problems. Marge finally asks the key question, "Can't we
just get a better bus?" and eventually the monorail concept is
exposed as an inappropriate solution applied to a community
that didn't need it in the first place. Publicly subsidized mass
transit is not an absolute precondition for good quality development, and most small to medium sized communities can
meet their mobility needs by combining walking, bicycling,
cars, trucks and buses - all of which travel on roads – combined
with sound land use planning. If we can learn to think in the
third mode, our highways vs. transit thinking will evolve beyond the current back- and -forth debate into sustainable forward motion.

# 2. THE TRANSPORTATION FOOD PYRAMID

## Learning from the Millennium

The connection between the public health and transportation professions has created a powerful force for change in the past decade. We are finally learning that driving to the gym and taking the elevator up to use a stair master might not make a lot of sense. Don't get me wrong, it's great to go to the gym and get some exercise – but we often solve one problem while at the same time creating another. Thinking in the third mode is about much more than transportation. It is about figuring out the connections between multiple types of problems and finding solutions that cut across the boundaries of conventional bimodal thinking. This can be seen in the common ground shared by transportation, infrastructure funding and public health.

If we could just think for a moment about how to address the issues of the national debate on healthcare within a sustainable framework, we would identify responses to major issues that can be solved using less energy, less money and at greater benefit to society. This perspective can be seen in the work of two parallel authors, Marcia Lowe of Worldwatch Institute, who wrote *"The Bicycle: Vehicle for a Small Planet"* and Frances Moore Lappé, who wrote *"Diet for a Small Planet."* Lappé's book made it clear that the energy required to feed a growing human population could not be sustainable if people continued to eat red meat, because that diet required too much energy to produce. Lowe's book made a similar argument that our transportation systems cannot be sustained if they are based on a large amount of travel being dependent on fossil fuels.

These two authors' ideas about food and mobility can be combined in the form of a 'transportation food pyramid' that bases mobility on utilizing the modes of travel that require the least energy as the base, just as the foods that require low production energy to produce (such as whole grains) serve at the base of the food pyramid. If we envision a transportation pyramid in this way, the most commonly used forms of mobility would be walking and bicycling, followed by buses, rail transit, cars and air travel as the modes increased in their demand for energy. People would generally be healthier if they used walking and bicycling as forms of transportation more often, especially if this were combined with a healthier diet based on a foundation of whole grain foods. To create this new mobility food pyramid requires third mode thinking to combine multiple issues into a new perspective.

Currently, there is a growing trend towards "Active Transportation," with significant work happening in Europe, Canada and the U.S. In many ways, Active Transportation is a re-packaging of advocacy for bicycling, walking and trails around the renewed interest in the connection between public health and public works. For example, initiatives such as Safe Routes to Schools are working to encourage transportation and public health officials to focus on building more walkable and bikeable communities around schools. President Obama's USDOT Secretary, Ray LaHood, (a Republican) became a national leader by promoting "livability" as a core issue, and there are new collaborations with organizations like the Robert Woods Johnson Foundation's Active Living by Design program.

Unfortunately, national policy has yet to capitalize on the potential to address transportation, environmental, safety, economic, health and energy issues at the same time. We still see distinct policy problems in silos, separated from each other by institutional, political and bureaucratic barriers. This makes it a huge challenge, for example, to integrate a third mode solution such as Active Transportation into the health care debate. It's difficult for these ideas to reach the top of the public policy agenda, even if they do cut across boundaries to provide multiple solutions. The greenways, trails and active mobility movements in the U.S. have historically worked at the edges of mainstream public policy, always trying to get on the national radar. Creating a new approach to these issues that utilizes third mode thinking at the individual, regional and national levels could help create a new transportation food pyramid.

My experience working in Washington, D.C. on the Millennium Trails project from 1998 to 2001 is an example of both the potential and the challenges to making this happen. At multiple levels, The Millennium Trails initiative was a highlight of my life. I had a rare chance to help take the trails movement in the U.S. to a new level, and it gave me a front-row ticket to the inside-the-beltway world at the end of the century. The Millennium initiative was only one step in the long story of the trails movement, and our success was built upon generations of volunteers and leaders who had helped create the vision of a national network of routes for people to walk, bike and use trails from border to border and coast to coast. The unique aspect of Millennium Trails was that we had a rare opportunity to put trails at the top of the national mobility pyramid.

In the late 1990s, the U.S. was very much aware of concerns about the "Y2K Problem" - computers' internal calendars might not be able to recognize the year 2000 and that glitch could cause major disruptions in electrical grids and computer systems when the clock struck midnight on New Years' Eve 2000. Billions of dollars were spent trying to solve this potential problem, and the Y2K computer issue overshadowed any idea of the year 2000 being an opportunity to create a national legacy. The Millennium program struggled to get the public's attention for a positive story and to overcome the perceptions of fear created by the Y2K problem. The message being sent to the general public at that time was to stock up on emergency supplies, bottled water and food in case there was a major crisis. Being prepared was equated with being in fear, being helpless in the face of a potential crisis, and hoping that somebody else solved the big technology problem for you. There were also plans for some pretty big New Year's Eve parties.

One of my personal solutions to the potential Y2K power failure issue was to stop using the elevator in our building. At that time my wife was seven months pregnant, we had two children under the age of six, and we lived on the top floor of a 12 story building. It was clear to us that if the power did go out, it would be up to me to go find food and supplies. At the beginning of the year, I started using the stairs to go down twelve floors to our building's basement gym. I'd often see my neighbors, who had taken the elevator to the gym, working out on the stair master machine. To me, this was a microcosm of modern society – people don't see the connections between the use of fossil-fueled energy and their own personal actions. After my workout, I'd run back up the twelve flights of stairs to our apartment. After doing this three times a week, I was starting to be in pretty good shape. After a couple of months, I was only using the elevator to go upstairs, and even then only if I was fully dressed for work in a suit and tie. By December, I was several pounds lighter and capable of going up and down the twelve flights of stairs easily.

On New Year's Eve, we attended the White House Millennium Concert and fireworks at the Lincoln Memorial. At midnight, the Y2K problem turned out not to be an issue – the power stayed on, the Metro was running, and we walked across the Potomac after spectacular fireworks – knowing that I had found a personal solution to a potentially serious problem. I have no idea what would have happened if the world's computers had failed at midnight. I can imagine a lot of people would have been trapped in their homes, unable to provide for their basic needs without emergency support from government and social service agencies. What I do know is that Y2K preparedness cost a lot of money to fix all those computers. Our nation missed a major opportunity to invest in other legacy projects, and to ask individual citizens to be a self-reliant part of the solution to national challenges.

The big New Year's Eve 2000 celebration on the Mall in DC was its own microcosm of my time in Washington. I was fortunate to get invited to join President Clinton and a thousand guests in the secured seating area at the Lincoln Memorial. The event was hosted by Will Smith, orchestrated by John Williams, and featured major stars including Quincy Jones. Our bleacher seating had access to a heated bar and rest rooms. Meanwhile, the nearly 500,000 people out along the National Mall were jammed around the edges of the reflecting pool, with big video screens. They couldn't see the stage because our bleachers were in the way.

At midnight, the televised program stopped for a few words from the President followed by a fireworks display over the Washington Monument. It lasted less than five minutes. The patriotic fireworks were enough to create a brilliant image in the global media. The video screens showed similar shots from the Eiffel Tower, Times Square and other landmarks. Meanwhile, the crowd on the Mall, disappointed at the brief live show, began to move away. Many of the Lincoln Memorial guests left shortly after, including a large group that went back for a private party at the White House.

We were left along with a small group of guests who stayed for the end of the show, and about 45 minutes later we were actually dancing on the stage and singing along with the performers. At one point, Quincy Jones came over to my wife, patted her pregnant belly and said, "It's going to be a great year to have a baby boy." Then at 1:00 am, a huge fireworks barge on the Potomac set off a fantastic fireworks show, and confetti canons blasted the stage with silver and gold stars. There were very few people left on the Mall to see this part of the show, but it probably looked great on TV. At so many levels, this memorable event symbolized a lot about life inside the Beltway at the end of the Millennium: a great show for the media that was amazing if you had access to the inside story, but a very different event for the general public.

The premise of Millennium Trails was that the trails movement in the U.S. was a vital part of the American legacy for the year 2000. The turning of the calendar would only happen once in a thousand years, so it seemed like an opportunity to try and take the trails movement to a new level in the U.S. In the U.K., the organization SUSTRANS was using a national Millennium Lottery to create a 10,000 mile national bikeway network. Other countries were developing similar initiatives to celebrate the year 2000. In early 1998, I had heard through contacts at some of the national trails organizations that the White House was considering ideas for new programs to commemorate the Millennium year. Fortunately, I had met one of the key people, Deputy Secretary John Horsley of the U.S. Department of Transportation (USDOT), at a conference the previous year. When I called John and told him about some of the great trail projects that were happening around the country, he recruited me to move to DC and run the program.

We knew that even a White House initiative would have a hard time trying to change the deeply held American love of the automobile and help make trails a mainstream part of the American landscape. At the same time, trails were an ideal opportunity to tell the story of America's past, present and future. The trails movement in the U.S. was growing, in many ways thanks to progressive federal transportation funding programs in the

1990's. USDOT was in a position to be a catalyst to shift our nation beyond the highways vs. transit paradox. A national trails initiative was a third mode way of connecting USDOT's programs and the trails movement's potential with the White House Millennium program.

We also knew that walking, bicycling and trails are powerful symbols of the potential to create healthy, safe, livable communities. The federal funding for trails was helping communities re-structure their transportation pyramids. Unfortunately, the reality of 20th century America had been centered on a monocultural approach to building an automobile-centered society. The result was that by 1998, levels of obesity were reaching epidemic levels, driven by historically high levels of physical inactivity. If a leader had come to America in the 1940s and said, "our goal as a nation is to build an infrastructure that makes it impossible for people to walk or ride their bikes," people would have said it was impossible.

American health data of the late 1990s showed that this was exactly what was happening. Children had stopped walking and bicycling to school – because it was no longer safe to do so in many communities. Adults had become commuters who drove to work every day, children had become passengers who were driven to every daily activity, and America had created an entire generation that lived in suburbs designed exclusively for the automobile. Television, video games and a variety of sedentary lifestyle activities had combined to create a population that was overweight and out of shape. For the first time since health data had been kept in the U.S., the current generation of Americans was likely to live a shorter lifespan than their parents. This was (and still is) a shocking statistic. There was no magic pill that could simply make Americans healthier – although plenty of people held out hope that this was possible.

Traditional methods of medical intervention were not going to solve this problem, and it would take a third mode solution to create a new infrastructure. The trails, bicycle, pedestrian and trails movement was gaining strength, but still fighting against the tide of the American Dream. Trails advocates had historically been volunteers, and had evolved along with the environmental movement of the late 1970s. In the mid-1990s they had begun to influence the world of transportation and infrastructure, and had begun to collaborate with broader coalitions. With the addition of the health community's involvement, it was possible to imagine trails gaining acceptance as a solution to a wide variety of critical issues. Getting these issues to the top of a nation's priorities is not an easy task, and I had a lot to learn when I arrived in Washington, D.C. in the spring of 1998.

One of the first things I learned was that when a leader really wants to make something happen, it's amazing how fast it gets done. When I first talked with John Horsley at USDOT about the potential Millennium Trails program, he asked me to write down my concept in two pages or less and send it back to him that day. What I didn't know was that the next week he was going to be at a White House briefing about the potential Millennium Trails initiative – and that those two pages were going to become part of his briefing package. In our first meeting, we had laid out a broad framework of getting national recognition for trails at the local, state and national levels. First Lady of the United States Hillary Clinton liked the concept, and USDOT

Secretary Rodney Slater agreed to support the initiative. A short time later I was asked to come back to DC as the Director of the U.S. Millennium Trails program.

I found Washington, DC to be everything people said about it: a very one-mode place where political power is the defining theme. The "inside the beltway" mentality was even more of a way of life than I had imagined. Fortunately, there were some remarkable people who consistently stayed above the power plays and they helped make Millennium Trails a successful program. They understood that trails had the potential to change the transportation food pyramid and become a lasting legacy for future generations – but only if we could get the trails movement up to a new level. Through this experience, I learned a lot about how third mode thinking can be applied to problem solving in a variety of very challenging situations at the national level.

In early discussions about the project, Millennium Trails had started with a somewhat esoteric concept of 'trails' as a metaphor for big ideas such as the 'Trail of Knowledge' and the 'Trail to Mars.' These were symbolic visions of the future, but they did not capture the real world vision of the trails movement in America. Great trails, like the Appalachian Trail, the East Coast Greenway, and the American Discovery Trail, were real projects that were shaping the American landscape. I knew that these on-the-ground, physical trails were the heart and soul of a great movement in our nation. That movement was often laboring in obscurity and needed a way to be seen at the national level.

A big part of my challenge in the early months of the project was to convince a core group of leaders that real-world trail projects were the key to creating a lasting legacy for the year 2000 at the national level. In my first weeks in DC, we worked with the USDOT leadership to develop a focused strategy for Millennium Trails: define the program, collaborate with the leaders of the trails movement in the U.S., identify a signature event to publicly launch the program, and then be able to announce major funding for projects by the end of the first six months. Each of these steps pushed me to learn how to work in, around and through a constantly shifting maze of opportunities and challenges.

It took a series of key presentations, including a meeting with Harriet Fulbright, who chaired the President's Council on the Arts and Humanities (PCAH), to get the project rolling. Fortunately, I had access to the PCAH Millennium working group meetings through USDOT's partnership with the White House Millennium Council. In my first meeting with the PCAH, I felt like a deer caught in the headlights. We met in Harriet's office in the Old Post Office Building on Pennsylvania Avenue. Wood paneling, traditional furnishings and a room full of high-level people. I was given a chance to make the case for real trails that people could walk and bike on as the focus of the Millennium Trails program.

Of all the people in the room, it was Harriet who put me at ease and supported the concept of focusing on real, physical trail projects and nominating local, state and national Millennium Trails as a way to connect the country. By the time the meeting was over, she had not only understood the new concept of the program, but she volunteered to help make connections in DC and New York that would be critical to our success. She clearly saw the potential in a new way of viewing an idea that was different from the initial concept proposed by the PCAH – and her leadership was a priceless resource throughout the project.

Setting up partnerships with the leadership of the U.S. trails movement was both a great joy and a real challenge. Since the trails movement is so diverse, there are a wide range of national advocacy organizations. These groups include the Rails to Trails Conservancy, American Trails, the American Hiking Society and others, as well as a full range of federal agencies including the USDOT, National Parks Service, US Forest Service and others – and each has its own interests. We established a national "Green Ribbon" panel of advisors for the Millennium Trails program to encourage support and communications among the diverse trail partners. We set up contracts with several of the nonprofit groups instead of using conventional consulting firms as a way to help them share in the opportunities of the Millennium initiatives. We all reported to the White House Millennium Council, which was headed by Ellen Lovell. She reported to both the First Lady and the President.

Once the Millennium Trails program structure was in place, my job became an epic task of managing multiple partners, with limited resources and fixed deadlines. At times I felt like I was on top of the world, at other times it was like herding cats. Our first key challenge was to create a launch event for the First Lady to publicly announce the program. I was tasked to find an event site, which to me seemed simple: I called David Dionne, director of the Anne Arundel County Trails Program in Maryland and chair of the East Coast Greenway. He immediately volunteered to host the event at his headquarters on the Baltimore-Annapolis (B&A) Trail. It was a location that captured the whole story of the trails movement in America: an abandoned rail line that had been turned from an eyesore into a community asset, with volunteers planting community gardens, a 'friends of the trail' organization led by a former NASA scientist (Stan LeBar, who helped design the camera for Apollo 11 that took the famous photo of Neil Armstrong walking on the moon), and a designated section of the future East Coast Greenway trail from Maine to Florida.

This probably sounds like an easy decision, right? The perfect story, a great location close to DC, a willing host for the event...but nothing was easy. Like so many other decisions in DC, this one wasn't simple. The White House Millennium Council didn't just say 'yes' to our recommended site. They required a full investigation of every other possible option within an hour's drive of DC. It took a week to visit multiple sites, meet with potential hosts and document the alternatives. While I understood the value of looking at options, I knew that we were using up a lot of valuable time and energy – and they eventually ended up agreeing that the B&A Trail was the right location for the event.

It's probably because the Millennium Trails kickoff on October 5, 1998 was my first event with the Washington DC "principals" that I remember so many details. What started as a simple photo-op and walk down the trail with First Lady Hillary Clinton, a boy scout and girl scout quickly mushroomed into a 1,000 person event including USDOT Secretary Slater, National Park Service Director Robert Stanton, members of Congress,

Governor Parris Glendenning and others. We needed a stage, shuttle buses, massive amounts of security, invitations, scripted speeches, media packets and a myriad of other details. What it took to get that event off the ground taught me a lot about how DC works.

The weeks leading up to the kickoff event were crammed with briefings, script writing and a maze of shifting details. A guest list had to be run through the White House security protocols in advance. As the scale of the event grew, the list was first increased, then it was limited to a strict number of guests, then at the last minute hundreds of extra people were invited to ensure we'd have a full crowd. At a pre-event run-through, the Secret Service told the sound technicians we had hired to leave because they weren't necessary. An hour later, during the same meeting, I was asked, "Where the hell are the sound guys?" because we needed them. They were called in their truck on the way back to their office and told to return to the site for the briefing.

Fortunately, in my first few months, I had learned to anticipate some of this stuff. On the day of the event, I had asked our graphics staff to make doubles of all the signs, posters, American flags and Millennium T-shirts we had ordered. As we were setting up the podium, I placed one of the Millennium Trails logo signs on the lectern. Two minutes later, a White House advance staffer came over and said he didn't like the lectern sign because the letters "Millennium Trails" were in vertical text, not horizontal. I told him we had already gone through this and the graphics had been approved by the Millennium Council. He insisted that we cut the sign with a razor knife and tape the letters horizontally below the logo. Our event staff was shocked – this was the key photo-op sign that the First Lady and other speakers would be standing in front of for the big event.

Since I knew that there was a second copy of the lectern sign, I offered to cut the one we'd put up with a knife as requested. Before I made the cut, I told the White House staffer that he would have to accept full responsibility for his decision if it turned out wrong. We were both sweating when I did it – the event was less than an hour away after a month of planning. I razor cut the sign, taped it back up on the lectern in two pieces as requested – and it looked much worse than before. The White House staffer panicked and started blaming my graphics team for doing a lousy job. I let him go on for a few minutes before I asked him if it had looked better before we cut it. He knew that it did, and was shocked when I went and got the extra backup sign and put it up on the lectern. It was just as we'd planned, and graphic looked great in the media coverage of the event.

There were literally dozens of these kinds of issues happening throughout the development of our program, and all of them required quick thinking to resolve. Our largest non-profit partner had been charged with producing the media packets, but there had been some issues with the content they had produced. In a meeting with the White House Millennium Program staff, we had realized that the packets included inaccurate information about the organization and its director. It had also been made clear that the order in which the speakers' bios were inserted in the packets had to follow official protocol, with the First Lady listed first, the USDOT Secretary next, etc – and with the non-profit partner last as a result. It wasn't a total surprise when the packets got handed out to the media at the kickoff event without these changes being made. We had to scramble quickly to have staff retrieve the packets and get them corrected. I learned that this was the kind of inside the Beltway egotism that made every event a challenge.

As the Millennium trails kickoff event unfolded, the original guest list of 400 had swelled to more than a thousand people. There were shuttle buses to remote parking areas, VIP seating passes, stage lighting and cameras. Behind the scenes, a major political drama unfolded, since the First Lady and Governor Glendenning were appearing in public for the first time since he had made some unfavorable comments about Presidential Clinton. Our small photo-op of the First Lady on a trail with a couple of kids ended up being a small parade, with a crowd of guests and enough media to get the story out nationally. The speeches were great, there were lots of kids smiling and waving flags in their Millennium Trails t-shirts – and by the end of the day we had successfully launched a new national program.

The program that made its public debut on October 5, 1998 became a two year odyssey though the "Inside the Beltway" world. As an outsider to the politics and power issues of Washington DC, I had a unique perspective and tried to use that as an advantage both for the success of the program and for my own sanity. Bear in mind that this was an unusual time – the President was being impeached, the First Lady was about to run an election campaign as a Senator in New York, and we were an underfunded initiative that was full of potential but unknown on the Washington priority list. Navigating these issues was a constant test of the ability to keep the success of the trails movement as our top priority. Our job was to be a catalyst for projects that might take years to develop, and to gain visibility for projects that had already been started by generations before us. The cat herding intensified as the program developed.

After the launch event, our next two major tasks were to establish a recognition program for trails at the local, state and national levels, and to identify projects that could receive funding through a national public-private partnership. The program structure was relatively simple: trails would receive designation as Community Millennium Trails based on submittals from local jurisdictions, state-level Millennium Legacy Trails were to be submitted by the Governors, and National Millennium Trails would be selected by the USDOT Secretary. The Rails-to-Trails Conservancy served as the primary organization to manage the application process. We held monthly "Green Ribbon Panel" meetings to support the process. This working group served in an advisory capacity to the USDOT and White House leadership team. Our initial goal was to get more than 2,000 projects designated as Millennium Trails.

The challenge of getting funding for the Millennium projects was another microcosm of the whole Beltway process. USDOT Secretary Slater and his team had identified an opportunity to utilize the Public Lands Highway (PLH) funding program for Millennium Trails. Bicycle, pedestrian and trail projects were eligible for PLH funds - if the projects were located on Federal public lands. However, no bicycle, pedestrian or trail projects had been previously funded by this program, largely due to the agency's historical bias towards conventional highway projects. I was given the task of finding $5 million in potential projects to fund from this source, and to provide a list for the Secretary to select from.

For me, this was an easy task. Through my network of contacts, I knew that there were plenty of potential trail projects on federal lands. Within a few days I had identified more than $20 million worth of projects in National Parks, National Forests, and on other federal lands. We quickly provided these eligible projects with the application materials that they needed, and offered support in producing high quality grant applications. When I met with the director of the PLH program to make sure he knew what we were doing, I was a little bit shocked but not completely surprised when he said: "you can't spend our money on those trail projects." I responded that I thought the PLH funds were taxpayers' money. He was just as shocked as I was, and we both ended up agreeing that by law, it was really up to the Secretary of Transportation to decide how the funds were distributed.

At the end of the month, it was clear that we had found more than enough eligible projects. Through a Memorandum of Understanding (M.O.U.) that had been signed between USDOT and the Department of the Interior, a collaborative initiative had been established for innovative transportation programs in signature National Parks including Yosemite, Grand Canyon, Acadia, Grand Teton, the Presidio and Yellowstone. It should have been easy for each of these places to get PLH funding for trails, but even that proved to be a challenge. Like most of our nation, the National Parks had focused their infrastructure efforts in the late 1900's on traditional highway projects.

Each of the M.O.U. Parks was given an opportunity to submit trails projects for the PLH funding. I even travelled to Yosemite to help them write their proposal – they had a great potential project to resurface the old bike paths in the Valley to bring them up to modern standards. We met with the non-profit Yosemite Fund, the Superintendent and his key staff and reviewed the proposal. We walked the trails in the valley, and spent a day looking at the possible conversion of an old rail line into a trail along the Merced River. I left thinking that Yosemite would become a great place for biking and walking as a result of the PLH funding, and even a model for the rest of the National Parks system. Unfortunately, when I got back to DC, I was told that the Park had decided not to submit the application. They felt that they already had enough other priorities, and did not want to take on a new project. This was a significant missed opportunity.

Ultimately, we did develop a great list of projects, and USDOT Secretary Rodney Slater awarded funds to trails that included the Erie Canal Trail at Fort Stanwix in New York, the Teton Pass Millennium Trail in Jackson Hole, Wyoming, the Grand Canyon Greenway in Arizona, the Presidio Trails system in San Francisco, and the Acadia National Park carriage trails in Maine. These projects represented the first time that the Public Lands Highway program had funded bicycle and pedestrian trail projects. When John Horsley made the funding announcement at the November, 1998 National Trails Symposium in Tucson, he presented a giant check to the Arizona delegation. I will never forget the image of the Arizona Trails leadership openly weeping at the sight of that check. They knew that this was a significant moment, and that decades of hard work had finally resulted in national recognition for the trails movement. At the same time, the battle to get other projects to follow this lead would continue for many years to come. Ultimately, the resistance to seeing walking, bicycling and trails as an integral element of our nation's transportation system was a bigger issue than Millennium Trails could solve.

The third phase of the Millennium Trails initiative was to fill in the structure of Community, Legacy and National Millennium Trails. The Green Ribbon Panel worked to get the word out and to encourage applications at each level. We were able to secure a major sponsorship from the American Express Company, and that money was targeted to the National level projects. Not surprisingly, politics ended up playing a significant role in the nomination process. Texas and New York (both of whom had Republican governors) declined to submit applications for the state-level Millennium Legacy Trails. I could almost understand Texas' decision since George W. Bush was Governor, but I was particularly disappointed by my home state of New York.

As the former State Bicycle/Pedestrian Program Manager, I knew that New York had great opportunities for trails. I had helped the New York State Canal Corporation with their PLH funding application for a section of the Erie Canal Trail – including meeting with the State's grant writer while I was home in Saratoga on vacation that summer. They had submitted the application at the last minute, but I noticed that the Erie Canal Trail had not ended up on the list compiled by USDOT. Fortunately for New York State, the proposal was added to the list and the project was awarded PLH funding. Unfortunately, even with this level of help, New York State's Republican political leadership kept the Erie Canal from gaining national recognition as a Millennium Trail because the First Lady (a Democrat) was running for the

Senate. The funding for the Erie Canal Trail through the Millennium Trails program was never formally acknowledged by New York State. Fortunately, with 48 other states, the District of Columbia, and Puerto Rico all participating, we did end up meeting our target of 50 Millennium Legacy Trails.

Meanwhile, back inside the beltway, we continued to develop the candidates for major projects that would be selected as National Millennium Trails, the signature projects of the entire program. Proposals had been requested from throughout the nation, and each trail was eligible to receive a grant through our corporate sponsor, the American Express Company. We were prepared to make the announcement at the Rails-to-Trails Conservancy's national Trails and Greenways conference in Pittsburgh, in the spring of 1999. This would be a major event, with USDOT Secretary Rodney Slater making the announcement. Each of the National Trails would be honored as the Trail of the Month during the Millennium Year, capping our initiative with a collection of truly visionary projects.

When Secretary Slater arrived in Pittsburgh, the media releases, website and related materials were all ready to go. The conference audience was thrilled by the announcement of 16 National Millennium Trails. The final list represented a complete cross section of our nation, with projects including the East Coast Greenway, the Mississippi River Trail, the American Discovery Trail, the Underground Railroad Trail, the Lewis and Clark Trail, the Appalachian Trail and ten others that symbolized our nation's past, present and future. We knew that these projects would, in some cases, take a generation - or more – to reach their goals. We also knew that we were making a rare attempt at creating a new legacy for future generations.

The Millennium Trails program was one of many times where it was a challenge to balance life and work in the course of my career. If I had learned anything during my time in Washington, it was that it's easy to lose yourself in the constant demands of work. At that time, technology and communications were making it possible to both be in constant contact and to find ways to keep work in its place. I found this out on multiple occasions, and constantly tried to find a way to maintain a balance between family, friends and work. This was a critical part of keeping my sanity and not having the pressures of work take over my entire life. I learned to value my time, my family and our lives as much as I did my work, and to make that balance a priority. Sometimes that meant doing the best you could, trusting other people to follow through, and knowing that you can't win all of the time.

On one occasion, I was at the U.S. Forest Service national training center in Shepherdstown, West Virginia, for an annual meeting of the National Trails System managers. As the meeting was ending on Friday afternoon (these things always seemed to happen on Fridays), I got a message regarding an event with the Vice President and the Transportation Secretary. They were travelling to an event in Derry, New Hampshire the following Monday. The Secretary's office wanted to know if there were any federally funded trail projects near the event location. I told them that it was already late in the day on a Friday, and I was in a conference center in West Virginia that only had a single dial-up internet connection, and it was in their library – but I would do my best. I went to the library, got online, searched out a contact I had met from New Hampshire DOT, and called him to see if there were any opportunities. I was surprised to catch him in his office on the first ring. He told me that there was an $800,000 federally funded rail trail project within a block of Main Street in Derry, New Hampshire.

I couldn't believe my luck. I quickly called back to DC and was able to provide enough information for key staff to develop a briefing package for the project site in New Hampshire. It was the perfect combination of the right project in the right place, and within an hour the information was on its way to the right people. We spent the weekend thinking that this would be a significant opportunity, especially since the Vice President was positioning himself as a major environmental leader and likely Presidential candidate. On Monday, the event took place as scheduled, but I was stunned when one of the advance people called me to say that the trail project never got mentioned. The event had focused on jobs and economic development, and even the presence of a federally funded trail construction project just a few blocks away wasn't meaningful enough for the VP's handlers to capitalize on the opportunity. This was yet another example of how challenging it was to get trails on the national radar. When the Deputy Secretary who had prepared the briefing package for the event left his job a few months later, he put that package on his desk so his successor could see how this kind of missed opportunity could – and did - happen.

Missed opportunities were not just a political issue within government during my time in DC. Keeping a partnership of America's national trail organizations all working together had its own politics and challenges. As with any national movement, there was a wide variety of trail organizations, and each had its own agenda. The Rails to Trails Conservancy was our biggest partner because they were the largest national membership organization, and their focus was on multi-use paths separated from the roads. Other groups such as the League of American Bicyclists, American Hiking Society, the Coalition for the National Trails System, and American Trails each had their own interests and constituencies.

I have tremendous respect for all of the organizations and their members who contribute their time, energy and money to help build trails in our country. At the same time, my experience in DC showed that there are egos, agendas and self-interests in the non-profit world that match their counterparts in government and the private sector. For example, at one point, one of the non-profits that was under contract for the Millennium Trails project was not meeting clearly defined deadlines for their deliverables. The White House Millennium Council made it clear that these deliverables were required, and after multiple attempts to get the work completed, the deadlines continued to slip. The Millennium Council agreed to have a meeting with USDOT and the non-profit's executive director. These were not easy meetings to schedule, and they were usually taken very seriously. It's not that often that any trail organization gets a chance to meet with staff from the White House and USDOT brass.

On the day of the meeting, the Millennium Council got a call from the non-profit's Executive Director, saying that he would be unable to attend because he was at the airport awaiting a flight to attend a conference in Europe. He said that he would be sending his organization's Vice President to the meeting instead. Within minutes, the Millennium Council had called USDOT and said the meeting had been cancelled. I was already in USDOT Deputy Secretary Gene Conti's office getting ready for the meeting when the call came in. I could not believe that the non-profit's director had caused the meeting to be cancelled. I was in the middle of battle of wills between a nonprofit that I have always supported and the White House, who we all depended upon for the success of our program. The nonprofit clearly did not have the power to win this battle, and was way out of line in a dozen different ways.

About a half hour after the meeting was cancelled, the nonprofit's Vice President arrived at the USDOT building and demanded to be allowed in to meet with the Deputy Secretary. When the security staff denied her access to the building, she called my cell phone, screaming that the meeting should not have been cancelled. She didn't know that I was in the Deputy Secretary's office when she called. It was an almost comical situation, if it hadn't been so tragic and carried such significance for the trails movement. If these were our friends, it was hard to imagine how our enemies would behave. The Deputy Secretary agreed to talk to her on the phone, only to have her scream at him just as loudly as she'd done to me. It took weeks to get the issues straightened out, get the contracts back on schedule and to have a follow-up meeting where we ultimately saved the Millennium Trails program from this ego-driven disaster.

After that meeting, I was given Congressman John Lewis's inspiring book about the Civil Rights movement, "*Walking With the Wind.*" In his book, Lewis describes the internal struggles within the leadership of groups that defined his generation.

While I wouldn't equate the struggle for Civil Rights with the future of the trails movement, I do think John Lewis tells a powerful story of what really goes on in a social movement, and how not all of what happens on the outside matches what is going on inside. That book helped me understand where Millennium Trails wasn't reaching its potential. In part because of our inability to get all the trails organizations working from the same page, we were ultimately unable to raise the kind of funding that should have been possible, and we ended up without the long term support that was generated for some of the other Millennium projects in the U.S. and internationally. In the end, Millennium Trails designated more than 1,000 projects, had more website hits than any other project of its kind at that time, and helped serve as a catalyst for some truly amazing initiatives – but I will always know that we could have done more.

At the end of President Clinton's term, I had been asked to extend my contract for an extra six months to help wrap up the Millennium Trails project. I moved my family back to upstate New York so my children could start school in September, and agreed to work from Saratoga through the end of the Presidential transition period. This turned out to be a good decision for my family, since the 2000 election turned into a nightmare of miscounted votes, hanging chads and an historic Supreme Court decision. Long after Election Day had passed, Washington was still in election chaos. It was at this point that one of my favorite DC moments happened.

Throughout the Millennium Trails program, we had been trying to create a more lasting legacy for the trails movement. One of our tasks to meet this goal was to try and get an Executive

Order on Trails signed by President Clinton. This had proved a very challenging task because The White House had a lot of other priorities during that time. The primary purpose of the Executive Order was to formalize the process for all the federal agencies to work together on trails. We had already helped strengthen an existing interagency working group, had drafted the Executive Order and had the USDOT and Interior Secretaries sign off on it, but it had stalled at that point. We still needed signatures from the USDA Forest Service, the Department of Health and Human Services and the Department of Education before the final version could be sent to the White House. As the Clinton Administration came to close, we were given one last minute chance to get the Executive Order approved.

Ellen Lovell of the White House Millennium Council did not want to give up on getting the order signed. I was at a meeting in DC on December 12th, 2000. We were preparing materials for the Presidential Archives, and Ellen called a staff meeting to say that we should make one more attempt at getting the Executive Order to the President's desk. We all knew it was a long shot, but she insisted it was still worth trying. We needed the signatures of three cabinet secretaries, and then she would have to get the document in front of the President for final approval. After we outlined our strategy, we had a break between meetings in the middle of the day. I decided to take a walk – and got a bonus view of an historic scene on Capitol Hill.

I walked up Pennsylvania Avenue to the Supreme Court to try and catch some of the ongoing drama of the Bush vs. Gore election decision. It was lunchtime, and there was the usual flow of people on the West Capitol Street sidewalk. Across the street from the Supreme Court, there was a mass of media crews, with their cameras trained on the façade of the Court. From their angle, the passing lunchtime pedestrians made it look like there was a big crowd across the street. At the same time, I could see that the steps in front of the Court were empty, and there seemed to be people walking in and out of the main entrance. Down at sidewalk level, there was only handful of protesters, including one in a memorable superhero costume waving a protest sign.

It was another very Washington moment – a great image for the media, but in reality there didn't seem to be much going on. I crossed the street, walked up the steps, went into the main lobby, and walked right up to the entrance to the empty Supreme Court chambers. There were visitors taking tours, and some curious onlookers like me hoping to find out about the election decision. I went down to the cafeteria and ate lunch, surrounded by staff from various media crews. What none of us knew was that the Court was meeting upstairs in a secret session. I left and walked back to work, and was at a hotel that evening when the Supreme Court announced that George Bush had been declared the next President of the United States.

It was a historically depressing time for at least half of the United States, but we still tried to put our plan for the Executive Order into motion. We now knew that there were only a few weeks before a major shift would take place in our national leadership's view of progressive issues like building trails. There was no way we could get anything done during the media storm that took place after the Supreme Court decision. We knew that there was at least one final opportunity for the President to make a statement about Millennium Trails: a ceremony scheduled in the East Room on January 17th 2001 to honor the 200th anniversary of the Lewis and Clark expedition. George Bush's inauguration was set for January 20th.

In the days prior to the Lewis and Clark event, we put our last minute plan into motion. We had a Millennium Council staffer go by taxi to each Cabinet Secretary's office with the original copy of the Executive Order. When he got to the front entrance of each building, we placed a phone call from the Millennium Council office to that Secretary's staff saying that a courier was on the way upstairs with a document that required immediate signature. It worked exactly as planned, and within a couple of hours we got the signatures we had needed for months. The signed original was brought back to the Millennium Council office and hand carried to the West Wing.

On January 17th, we still had not heard if the Executive Order had been signed. We hoped that there would be an announcement at the Lewis and Clark event. The Lewis and Clark Trail was one of the 16 National Millennium projects, and we had submitted talking points to the speechwriters. The East Room filled with guests, and President Clinton presided over a ceremony that captured the potential symbolism of the White House. It was 200 years to the day from when Thomas Jefferson had met with Lewis in Clark in the same East Room. President Clinton held in his hands a compass that had been used on the original expedition. The descendants of Lewis, Clark, Sacagawea and York were given honors that they had never fully received in their lifetimes. The symbolism was extraordinary –

but the Executive Order was never mentioned.

I left the room feeling an incredible mix of emotions. The powerful ceremony had captured the vision of trails in American history, but at the same time it had not fully connected with the idea of creating a new legacy through the White House Millennium Trails program. I left DC the next day and went home thinking that we had accomplished a lot of what we had set out to do, but that in spite of our best efforts, we still had not done everything we could have. I'm sure that is true for a lot of similar efforts. We had set our sights on 2,000 projects and ended up with 1,000. We had clearly taken the trails movement to a new level, but it not yet become a part of the mainstream. We had raised more than $10 million dollars for the program, but had watched while the U.K. used a national lottery to fund a $100 million dollar program that built a 10,000 mile national trails system.

Still, as the great Yogi Berra once said, "it aint over 'till it's over." In the chaos of the final days of the Clinton presidency, I got a call on Friday morning, January 19th from the Millennium Council saying, "he signed it." I said, "who signed what?" It was hard to believe, but I was informed that on January 19, his next-to-last day in office, President Clinton had issued Executive Order 13195: *Trails for America in the 21st Century*. There was no formal signing ceremony, and nobody had a final signed copy. In fact, it was almost impossible to confirm that it had been issued, since most of the White House phone lines and computers got shut down that day. It had been signed on January 18th, the day after the Lewis and Clark event at the White House. The Executive Order encouraged federal agencies to cooperate with communities and trail organizations to "protect, connect, promote, and assist trails of all types throughout the United States." It was published in the *Federal Register* / Vol. 66, No. 15 / Tuesday, January 23, 2001 / Presidential Documents, and is still in effect today.

It is interesting to look back at those events with a decade's worth of perspective. America in the year 2000 was a nation of optimism and hope. Our economy was humming along, the government was running a surplus, and initiatives like the White House Millennium program had a chance to create a positive legacy for the future. We may not have accomplished all that we could have, and we probably missed some opportunities, but we did create some lasting changes. We didn't know that within a year, the tragic events of 9/11 would send America into a decade of fear and war. In a way, my time spent working on Millennium Trails taught me that the third mode exists in time as well as being part of our physical infrastructure. We can't accomplish everything we want all at once, and some of our efforts may take years, decades, or generations to reach their full potential.

In addition to not capitalizing on the historic opportunity presented by the Millennium, it made me question why more people aren't encouraged in times of real or potential crisis – or in a rare moment such as the turning of a new century - to find a way to be part of the solutions to contemporary issues instead of being part of the problem. We spent so much money on the Y2K problem that we never really paid attention to the Millennium opportunity. We were trapped into thinking that the only possible solution was to spend more than $200 billion dollars on Y2K computer upgrades. As it turned out, maybe all that spending did work to prevent a global computer system meltdown - or maybe we spent a lot of money on something that wasn't a big issue at all.

All of the hype about the Y2K problem made people fear the New Year and kept us from using the turning of the calendar as a time to create a lasting national legacy. Don't get me wrong, I'm not an expert on the internal clocks of computers, but I do think the ability to create an opportunity to change the built environment of a nation may only come along once in a lifetime. If we had spent even half as much on the Millennium Program as we spent on Y2K preparedness, we could have built some really amazing projects. There is power in thinking about different ways to solve problems, and the Y2K story points out that the way we define an issue has a huge impact on the solutions we pursue. The U.K. defined the Millennium as a time to build major projects of lasting public value, including their 10,000 mile national bike route system. In the U.S., I hope we don't have to wait another 1,000 years to realize that trails still provide an opportunity to combine health and active transportation as potential solutions for a new mobility pyramid.

More than a decade after the Millennium project, I attended President Obama's inauguration in Washington, D.C. and saw this kind of thinking taken to a new level. The National Mall was a car-free zone, and all the surrounding streets were opened for people walking and bicycling. I flew from Albany to Baltimore at 6:00am that day, hoping to meet friends in front of the Washington Monument. I took a bus from BWI airport to the DC Metro at Greenbelt, joined the massive crowds getting on the trains, waited for more than an hour to get on board, and arrived at L'Enfant Plaza station by 10:00am. I stopped for a hot breakfast and strolled along with the joyous crowd down

Independence Avenue. I made it to the Monument by 11:00 am, only to find the crowd too packed-in to reach my friends. I ended up at the axis point between the White House, the Lincoln Memorial, the Jefferson Memorial and the Washington Monument. I will never forget standing on that spot, hearing President Obama begin a new era in American history.

It was after the inauguration that I enjoyed a rare third mode experience. Since my friends were on bikes and I had arrived on foot, I decided to meet them across the river in Arlington for dinner. The Metro system was jammed, but the major roads and bridges were still car-free, so I walked down the Mall, past the Lincoln Memorial and across the Theodore Roosevelt Memorial Bridge with thousands of happy people. The views across the Potomac to the Iwo Jima Memorial and the Capitol were stunning in the late winter sunshine – especially since the Roosevelt Bridge is an interstate highway. It is usually very difficult crossing that bridge on foot or by bike – there is only a narrow sidewalk on one side of the bridge. I walked all the way to Rosslyn before I got on the Metro, and avoided the motorized traffic and crowded train stations along the way. The first day of the new Presidency started well from my perspective. I wish that we could learn from that experience, and from the Millennium, how active transportation can move our nation every day.

# 3. THE FOUR LAYERS:

## NYC Greenways

Since the early 1990s, New York City has been developing a remarkable 350 mile urban greenway system. This system, combined with hundreds of miles of on-street bikeways, thousands of miles of sidewalks and access to the largest transit system in the U.S., will create a new model of urban mobility. This green infrastructure will make it possible for people to walk and bike throughout the City in new ways that support health, environmental, energy and economic development goals. The system has been the work of many hands, over many years, including public, private and non-profit partners. It is interesting that the system was not fully recognized as a complete infrastructure for many years, and it has taken a long time to get built, because the City's political and business leadership did not initially see its full potential as a new mobility system.

The New York City Greenways system is an extraordinary accomplishment. Even at a cost of $1 million per mile, the whole system could have been built as a single project for $350 million – or roughly one third of the annual transit or highway budgets for the region. I was fortunate in the mid-1990s to work with a group of innovative planners, advocates and leaders who helped develop the vision for this growing new green infra-structure. As New York State's bicycle and pedestrian program manager in 1993, I was asked to chair a task force called the Metro NYC Bikeway/Walkway Working Group (BWWG). My boss at NYSDOT told me that my mission was to "go down to the City and get as much money spent on bike projects as you can before anyone finds out what they're doing." The next week, I took the train down from Albany to Manhattan with Ivan Vamos, Deputy Commissioner of the NY State Office of Parks, Recreation and Historic Preservation (OPRHP), to attend my first meeting.

Ivan had started the BWWG along with a core group who real-ized that the landmark 1991 federal transportation legislation called "ISTEA" (the Intermodal Surface Transportation Effi-ciency Act) had made bicycle and pedestrian facilities eligible for federal funding. The working group had started meeting at OPRHP's offices to discuss possible opportunities. During our spectacular early morning train ride down the Hudson River, Ivan told me about every bike and pedestrian project in the State. He had led OPRHP's effort to purchase the abandoned Penn Central railroad line from Albany to Buffalo, making it possible for the future development of the 325 mile Erie Canal Trail. He had been a champion for the proposed Hudson River Greenway trail from Albany to New York City. When we walked into the meeting, Ivan introduced me by saying, "this is Jeff, he's the new bike guy at State DOT, and since I'm retiring next month, he'll be chairing these meetings from now on."

I was as surprised as everybody else in the room, especially since Ivan hadn't mentioned anything about his retirement or my new role on the train that morning. Meanwhile, at that first meeting I asked a simple question that changed the group's potential: "Why are we meeting at Parks when all the money is in transportation?" I made a few calls and arranged for the group's future meetings to be held at the New York Metropolitan Transportation Council (NYMTC), on the 82nd floor of the World Trade Center. NYMTC was the metropolitan planning organization responsible for programming federal transportation funding for the New York City region. They were required by ISTEA to have a bicycle and pedestrian plan. If the famous bank robber Willie Sutton had been involved in public works, he might have said you have to be in transportation, because "that is where the money is."

For the next five years, that group of people met at NYMTC on the first Wednesday of each month from 10:30 am – 1:00 pm. We helped develop and program more than $100 million dollars worth of bicycle, pedestrian and trail projects to form the core of the New York City Greenways system - before anyone knew what we were doing. The BWWG was comprised of a wide variety of advocacy organizations, public agencies, and interested citizens. There were more than 60 people on the core participants' list, and most meetings had at least 20-30 people in attendance. The working group had no official sanction or formal appointments to do what we did – in fact the group didn't even become a formal committee of NYMTC until the late 1990s.

That lack of formal authority may have been a key to our success. We simply agreed to coordinate efforts among a variety of interests with the common goal of getting funding approved for bicycle, pedestrian and trail projects. My job was primarily to play center field (which I had done in my Little League baseball career), keeping everyone informed via our meeting minutes, which were sent to all the attendees and elected officials in a simple, double-sided, one-page format. There was a constant debate about what types of projects should get funded – restriping crosswalks, putting in on-street bike lanes, and building waterfront greenways were among the options. By defining all these projects as part of the evolving regional Greenways system, we were able to get a wide variety of new infrastructure on the map.

For the BWWG meetings, I would leave home in Saratoga, drive to the Albany train station for the 7:00am express down the Hudson River, get in to Penn Station, switch to the subway, get out at Chambers Street / World Trade Center station, go up to the lobby, go through security, take the elevators up to the 82nd floor, and arrive in time for the meeting without having gone outside all morning. I often got there before people who were just walking over from City Hall. Since the conference room was an interior space, I always took the time to go into an office by the windows to enjoy the view before our meetings. Unfortunately, in all those times I was in the building, I never went to the observation deck or the Windows on the World restaurant, because they were in the other tower. It is still hard to be in Manhattan and know that the World Trade Center is gone. I believe that the BWWG's work to get the Greenways system to happen is a living memorial for the City.

While New York was in the early stages of creating its new green infrastructure, other regions were pursuing similar visions. In the early 1990s the regional plan for Metro Toronto was entitled *The Sustainable Metropolis*. It projected a growing metro region of three million people, yet at the same time included a concerted effort to expand the role of human powered transport. The region's river valleys were established as greenways, with walking and bicycling paths connecting down through the city. At the waterfront, these facilities connected to the Waterfront Trail, which provided non-motorized access at a regional scale. The city's leaders had made it possible to ride a bicycle throughout most of downtown Toronto on an innovative network of on-street bike lanes and paths, supplemented by an extensive supply of bicycle parking. While this system did not extend to the far reaches of Toronto's suburbs, at that time the core network was impressive when compared to New York and most of its North American counterparts.

In the 1990s, Toronto's civic leaders had striped a blue and green centerline of the future Waterfront Trail through parking lots, across the facades of abandoned buildings, over fences and on existing roads. As new sections of the trail were built, the blue and green colors were used on maps, signage and as the centerline of completed sections the Waterfront Trail. During that same period, Toronto implemented some very innovative on-street bicycle facilities. On Bay Street in front of City Hall, the city provided a shared bicycle, bus and taxi lane – creating a new form of shared urban street in the process. When the city switched from coin-operated parking meters to new electronic meters, the old posts were converted into "post and ring" bike racks to create thousands of new parking spaces for bicyclists.

In the last decade, as metropolitan Toronto expanded to become a regional government, the political power of the region has shifted to include the ring of sprawling suburbs surrounding the downtown area. In Toronto's 2011 council elections, the suburban voters became so strong that both of the candidates for Mayor became vocally anti-bike. When the new Mayor took office, one of his first promises was to remove the existing bike lanes from several key downtown streets. Local advocates were struck by the power of the anti-urban forces, and one response was an advertisement on E-Bay for "one slightly used urban bike lane, free to a city that can use it." This regressive step is part of the ongoing challenges of moving the world's growing metropolises into the future. Toronto had once been a model for new mobility, and it probably will return soon to its place as an innovative leader. Montreal has now taken the lead as the progressive mobility leader in Canada, with innovations including a network of new protected bike lanes that separate bicyclists from motorized traffic, the province-wide Velo Quebec bicycle touring route system and the innovative BIXI bike sharing system.

It is the cities of Europe, especially in the Netherlands, Germany, Spain and Denmark which have come closest to achieving a truly green infrastructure. Most European city centers are compact and pedestrian-oriented by historic factors of their development. American cities are young by comparison, and are like adolescents who haven't fully decided what to be when they grow up. Cities like Copenhagen, Amsterdam, Seville and Paris have mastered the art of moving people and goods with a minimum of fossil fuel and a maximum of fun. As a result, levels of walking and bicycling in these cities are more than ten times the mode share of most American cities. Suburban sprawl is happening in Europe and it will be important in the next decade not to repeat the mistakes of American style mono-modal development patterns.

It is extraordinary to experience the great Dutch towns such as Delft, Amsterdam and Utrecht. People of all ages and abilities interact, bicycling to school with their children, going grocery shopping without a car, and commuting along the canals and dykes. Most neighborhoods have high quality facilities for walking and bicycling. There are beautiful waterfront paths, busy pedestrian shopping streets, the train stations have bike rental and repair shops, and almost every street has a bike lane. Physical fitness, energy conservation, reduced air pollution and a very high quality of life are all made possible by this green infrastructure.

Unfortunately, most metro regions in the U.S. have not achieved these levels of green infrastructure development. Existing conditions in many American cities generally include disconnected pieces of a greenway network, but not completed systems. While the landmark transportation acts of 1991 and 1998 started providing significant resources, the ideal of fully connected greenway systems is far from reality in most U.S. cities. Denver, Chicago, San Francisco, and other cities have ambitious programs in progress, but they are still years away from completion at their current pace. This reality is combined with existing suburban sprawl and fossil-fuel based transport systems that continue to create an environment in which walking and bicycling have a very hard time competing with other transport modes. Many cities in the U.S. continue to debate the future of transportation as a battle between highways and transit, leaving green infrastructure solutions on the fringe of the issue.

At the same time, progress is happening, and it is incredible to think back on the New York City of the 1990s and realize that the world class bicycle, pedestrian and greenway infrastructure being implemented now did not exist then. The 1993 New York City Greenways Plan (produced by Karen Votava and her team at the Department of City Planning, in cooperation with Dave Lutz of the Neighborhood Open Space Coalition and other participants in the BWWG) was a completely new vision for the City. I think that the Greenways Plan is one of the greatest planning documents of all time – especially its simple graphic map that, for the first time, showed a clear vision of the entire system. It is hard to imagine a single sheet of 8 ½ x 11 paper that has had a greater impact. Also, at that time, the advocacy group Transportation Alternatives produced the Bicycle Blueprint for New York City, calling for an extensive network of bike lanes, bike parking and transit access improvements. In addition, a new group called Walk NY was trying to make sure that pedestrian facilities were an equal priority. Getting all of these concepts to work together was a significant challenge. It was during my work with the BWWG that I began to understand how important a variety of types of bicycle and pedestrian facilities would be for New York or any other city. I realized that the challenge wasn't to decide between which types of projects were most important, but how to get all of them to work together as layers in a complete system. This was particularly evident in the many battles over funding between the various interest groups. I once had to intercept a letter to the NYSDOT Commissioner from a well-known on-street bicycling advocate, urging the state to vote against funding the West Side Greenway because it was a waste of money that could be better spent on low-cost bike lane projects. At one point, when we tried to get all the pedestrian crossings re-striped as a city-wide project, the Metropolitan Transit Authority didn't want what they saw as 'their' money being spent on pedestrians (even though we agreed to do the crosswalks at bus stops first and most transit customers are pedestrians). Everybody had an agenda, and it was a challenge to maintain forward progress.

It's hard to believe how much opposition there once was to ideas that are now becoming more mainstream. So much of the noise that goes on gets lost and forgotten, and maybe that's a good thing. For example, I remember a series of debates with agencies like the Sanitation Department, who insisted that garbage trucks had to be parked on the West Side waterfront, or with the Police Department officials who insisted that the City's vehicle impound lot had to be located on the decaying piers in Chelsea. Even local neighborhoods in Greenwich Village opposed the Greenway along the Hudson River. This area has now become some of the most valuable waterfront real estate in the world. The garbage trucks and impounded cars were relocated to more appropriate locations.

At one point, there was a vocal outcry by opponents of the Greenway system that centered on the environmental damage that would be caused by building the system. The journal Urban Outdoors reported the following exchange in an August, 1999 story entitled "HUDSON RIVER GREENWAY OPPOSED":

*"Perhaps feeling empowered by compromises forced elsewhere in the City's 350-mile greenway system, people who call themselves environmentalists have announced opposition to construction of the Hudson*

*River Greenway in Riverside Park north of 96th Street. They claim that the asphalt path will cause runoff of pollutants into the Hudson River. They fail to notice that baby carriages, cyclists and skaters do not pollute any more than pedestrians and therefore do not create river-fouling hydrocarbons. "The greenway provides recreational opportunities in a city that sorely needs them, notes George Kaplan, former president of the NY Cycle Club. Park administrators have to make a value judgment about the validity of claims."*

As we fought through these battles and the various agencies had finally started getting projects on the ground, we attempted to get a more formal program established. I used up some political capital at NYSDOT to get a discussion about the future of the Greenway system on the agenda for the Program, Finance and Administration Committee (PFAC) at NYMTC. This was the organization's policy board, and featured powerful players including the NYC MTA and the region's elected officials. They met quarterly, and getting on the agenda was no easy task. I asked two key bike advocates to make the presentation, and provided a bulleted white paper of the key talking points – each tied to the PFAC acronym. We hoped to get comprehensive program established (P), dedicated funding for bike and pedestrian projects (F), staff hired to administer the program (A) and the BWWG formally established as a NYMTC committee (C).

Unfortunately, that meeting coincided with a major snowstorm, and my trip to the train station in Albany took more than three hours that day. I missed the 7:00am train, then the 8:00am train and the 9:00am train. I finally gave up and went to my office in Albany. I sent the "PFAC" talking points to a contact at the meeting, but the summary was never used by the advocates making the presentation. Instead, the powerful PFAC was given a slideshow about the potential vision for bicycling in New York City, and they weren't asked to do anything specific. It was a huge missed opportunity. There was nothing I could do to change the outcome of the meeting, and it probably set our efforts back a full year. I swore that day that if my worst commute was going to take three hours to go 35 miles, then I would bike to work from Saratoga to Albany on Bike to Work Day. I did, and it turned out to be the best day of commuting of each year that I worked in Albany.

On a lighter note, that year included one of my favorite all time New York City moments. We had finally found funding to hire a bicycle coordinator at NYMTC to support the working group. I had met a great candidate in Canada, named Ben Gomberg. He was working in London, Ontario at the time, and wanted a shot at working in the Big Apple. Ben had walked up to me after I spoke at a conference in Toronto, and said he was the right person for the job. We ended up talking over dinner at the Squeeze Club on Queen Street, where the conference organizers were holding a reception and getting ready to watch the Toronto Blue Jays' World Series game that night on a big screen. Around 7:30 pm, I told Ben that I was going to go to the stadium and try to scalp a ticket instead of watching the game on TV.

Ben thought I was crazy, and said he'd follow me on the subway down to the Skydome, because there was no way I'd get in to the game, and that way he'd have more time to talk with me on the way back to the bar. Just as we got to the stadium it started raining, and there were lots of scalpers stuck with tickets they couldn't sell. I bought two tickets – one for each of us – and went to the World Series with somebody I only met a few hours before. By the time the game was over, I knew that Ben was a great candidate for the New York City job.

When I got back to Albany, we arranged interviews for candidates, and when he applied for the position I agreed to meet with him in New York before his interview. That afternoon, I borrowed a bike from NYCDOT Commissioner Lee Sander, and took Ben on a tour of some of the new facilities being built in the City. In the evening, I had arranged for us to meet a friend from ABC News to talk about some new applications of satellite mapping technologies and to further encourage Ben to move to New York. We met at an outdoor café along Broadway across from Lincoln Center.

It was a warm summer evening, and we locked our bikes against the railing of the café right next to our table. We were enjoying our meal when I looked up and saw a thief on a beat-up old bike stop in front of us, pop the quick release on the Commissioner's bike, steal the seat and head off uptown on Broadway. Since nobody else stopped him, I jumped the railing and started running uptown to catch the thief. It wasn't my bike, and I couldn't imagine bringing it back the next day without the seat. The thief was riding uptown and weaving in and out of the bumper to bumper stream of yellow taxis headed downtown. He looked like a salmon swimming upstream, and I knew that at some point he'd have to turn around and head my way.

When the thief finally looped around and headed back towards me, I angled towards him and cut off his route downtown. He rode straight at me and held out the seat in one hand. I stepped aside, grabbed his wrist and threw him off the bike. He crashed to the ground, the seat popped loose, and I picked it up and ran back towards the café. I got a standing ovation and the maitre d' offered to pay for our meal. There was a police car nearby, but they were dealing with a man on the sidewalk who looked like he's lost a bar fight, and they offered no help. This was such a classic New York moment of the 1990s that it could have been a Seinfeld episode. When I brought the Commissioner's bike back the next day, I left him a note that said, "I saved your seat last night." Ben did not end up taking the job in New York City, but he did end up moving to Chicago, where he has served as that city's bike coordinator for the past 15 years.

Bear with me for one more New York Greenways story. The origins of the NYC Greenways system are based on the work of Frederick Law Olmsted, who invented the term 'parkway' to describe the landscaped boulevards he envisioned to connect Central Park, Prospect Park and other key destinations in the City. In fact, when the 1993 Greenways plan was developed, part of the concept was to connect remaining sections of the Olmsted Parkways and a network of bike paths built by Robert Moses during his reign as the City's master builder. Moses didn't like mass transit, but he had started building a network of new parkways in the 1960s – and they included both soft surface walking paths and paved bike paths.

In the 1990s, it turned out that Olmsted's Ocean Parkway was due to celebrate its 100th birthday. It is one of the oldest paved bike paths in the United States, and was worthy of a celebration. An event was planned with the New York City Parks

Commissioner, and he agreed to conduct a wedding for a young couple who would arrive on a tandem bicycle as part of the ceremony. We tried to get David Letterman to include the event on his show, but that did not work out. On the day of the event, in front of a crowd of Greenway supporters, the Commissioner was beginning the wedding ceremony when two motorists crashed their vehicles into each other on the adjacent Parkway. As the smoke and steam cleared, one of the drivers stepped out of his car, and the Commissioner recognized him from the podium. The driver was a local Brooklyn council member, and he was invited up onto the stage to join in the celebration while his car got towed away. It was a shame that the event wasn't televised on the Letterman show.

As the great humorist Dave Barry would say, you can't make this stuff up. Especially in a city the size of New York, it's amazing how much can happen without becoming part of the mainstream of media and politics. Over time, the Greenways system ended up following the three great stages of any new idea: total opposition, grudging acceptance, and then the opposition claiming credit for the whole thing having been their idea in the first place. The debates, plans and projects took place far below the City's radar, and just as my boss had predicted, millions of dollars were being spent and very few people were aware of it.

Mayor Dinkins released the original Greenways Plan, and it was unclear from his public statements at the time if he had ever read it. I once asked Mayor Giuliani on the podium at the start of the Great Five Boro Bike Tour if he knew about all the new projects under construction for the Greenway System, and he said 'no.' In fact, Giuliani signed a demolition order for the High Line elevated railroad in lower Manhattan – a landmark that has recently been transformed into one of the city's iconic new greenways. It took more than a decade for enough momentum to build, and for historic events to create the opportunity for the Greenway system to become front page news. I am honored to have played a small role in helping this effort, and thankful for the many people (most of whom never got credit for their great work) who helped make it happen.

On September 11, 2001, terrorists destroyed the World Trade Center. The new Hudson River Greenway along the West Side became an evacuation route, and the City's new waterfront esplanades served as staging areas for emergency services. There were news stories about executives going into bike shops in Manhattan, buying any bike available and asking for a good map so they could ride home. In the aftermath of the tragedy, there was a lot of talk about businesses leaving the City for safer places. In January, 2002, Mayor Bloomberg gave his annual State of the City address. He mentioned a handful of key priorities for rebuilding New York. The Greenway system was one of them. In the City's darkest hour, he knew that people needed a vision of hope, and a real solution that the City could accomplish quickly. In a great moment of leadership, he chose to take his City into a future shaped by green infrastructure.

Mayor Bloomberg called for the partially developed Greenway around the perimeter of Manhattan to be completed quickly. He had brought in Janette Sadik-Khan as his Transportation Commissioner, and she led an effort to implement the Greenways system and add more than 200 miles of bike lanes on the

City's streets. She brought in advisors from Amsterdam, Copenhagen and other progressive cities, and created a new plan for "Sustainable Streets." After years of attempts to push these ideas forward, changes suddenly began to happen with increasing speed. In a bold 'experiment,' Broadway was converted into a pedestrian street from Times Square to Herald Square. This was a logical idea, since Broadway is a diagonal street that cuts across the City's grid, creating complex intersections at multiple locations. The idea wasn't new and had been talked about by engineers and planners for many years.

In order to work around the cumbersome approval processes required for these major projects, the new pedestrian plazas were implemented as "interim" experimental projects that could be evaluated after one year. By using simple interventions such as signage, pavement markings, removable bollards, planters and street furniture, the City transformed Broadway from an urban traffic sewer back into one of the world's greatest streets. When you sit at a café table in the middle of Times Square today, it is hard to imagine that priceless public space being wasted in a traffic jam of motor vehicles just a few short years ago.

The difference with Mayor Bloomberg and his predecessors was that his team was able to implement real solutions that worked by using innovative, third mode thinking. He believed in the rational arguments in favor of making Broadway a great place for people by removing the cars. Yes, it was counterintuitive in a culture where the automobile is a national icon, and where many advisors believed the whole city would descend into chaos if even one lane of motor traffic was removed.

Fortunately, the 'experiment' worked. Ground floor retail space along the new pedestrian streets has become very valuable, people are walking and bicycling more, and all modes of traffic are moving smoothly through the simplified intersections. The new greenways, pedestrian plazas and bike lanes have redefined New York City. Unlike Bill Murray's prediction in Ghostbusters, the Mayor's decisions did not lead to "dogs and cats sleeping together" and panic in the streets. By thinking in the third mode, New York City is proving that new ideas for integrated mobility are critical for modern cities.

In order to implement a complete green infrastructure for transportation, communities need to have similar visions for complete systems of non-motorized transport. Whether you live in a metropolis like New York or in a small town, the network for walking and bicycling has to be a complete, integrated system in order get people out of their cars. This cannot be accomplished by providing a few isolated bike lanes, building a path along the waterfront, or converting an abandoned rail line into a trail. Don't get me wrong, these are good things to have, but by themselves they will provide little more than a place for recreation. While well intended, in many communities stand-alone trail facilities are often used by people who drive their cars from home to the local bike path, go for a ride and return to the car. This continues the use of short-distance motor vehicle trips, and the pollution caused by these trips in the car may offset any personal fitness gains realized by a ride or jog on the trail.

A complete green infrastructure for sustainable mobility is based on four layers of facilities: 1) greenways, 2) on-street bicycle facilities, 3) pedestrian sidewalks and crossings and 4) intermodal connections. When each of these individual layers is complete, and when all four layers are interconnected, is it possible to shift mobility into the third mode. Each of these layers can be described in detail as follows:

**Greenways** are the first layer of green infrastructure. Greenways are linear open spaces which include paths or trails for walking, bicycling and other non-motorized uses. In general, they should be developed on their own rights of way, independent of the road system. Greenways work best along waterfronts, rivers, abandoned railroads, utility corridors and other linear routes which serve to connect destinations. Trail surfaces can range from paved urban paths to stone dust or natural soil trails where appropriate. In some cases, shared-use trails can be developed along highway corridors and roadways, but ideally these facilities are clearly separated from motorized traffic and there should be limited intersections or crossings of adjacent land uses.

A person should be able to travel continuously along a greenway system with the same ease and consistency as a motorist on the highway. Intersections should be clearly signed, distances to the next destination identified, and rest areas, drinking fountains and benches provided at appropriate locations. It should take no more than 15 minutes travel by bicycle from any home in a community to reach the nearest greenway or trail. This is consistent with the national "Trails For All Americans" study developed in the 1990s, and provides a logical framework for establishing distance and destinations.

**On-street bicycle facilities** are the next layer of green mobility infrastructure. Nested within the network of Greenways, these facilities include bicycle lanes, signed bike routes and shared roadways, along with bicycle parking facilities. Every street and road in a community is part of this layer. Without these facilities, people simply can't get from their homes and businesses to other destinations. It is not possible to build a trail to everyone's front door, but nearly every house and business is located on a street. The key to understanding how to implement this layer lies in knowing the wide variety of potential on-street bikeway facility types, understanding where they belong, and maintaining a commitment to integrate them into literally every street and road.

The three factors which have the most significant effect on which type of bicycle facility are the width of space available to bicyclists, the speed of motor vehicles and the volume of motorized traffic. Other factors are also important, such as the condition of the roadway pavement, the presence of hazards such as potholes and storm grates, intersection conditions, the number of driveways entering the roadway and truck traffic volumes, but these are not as critical in most cases. Several formulas and models exist for evaluating these conditions, but in general it is possible to look with a trained eye at almost any road and determine whether a bike lane, signed route or shared roadway will be the appropriate choice. Innovative variations on these facility types include bicycle boulevards and cycle tracks, which combine aspects of traffic calming, wayfinding and trail design. The on-street bikeway layer is completed with the addition of good quality bike parking, including both short term racks and longer term lockers or covered parking areas.

It is amazing, but these simple design features are the basics of what is needed in terms of on- street bicycling infrastructure.

Bicycle lanes are among the most cost effective ways to improve non-motorized travel. In many American cities, roads have been over-designed with extra capacity and the space exists for on-street bikeways on many high-volume and suburban streets – the places where bicycling has the greatest potential. The term 'road diet' has emerged to describe the conversion of available street width into bike lanes. What is equally amazing is how reluctantly these conversions have been implemented, and the opposition that exists in the face of those who try to put them in place. We are talking about a battle for space on America's streets, and the prevailing mentality is that these streets were built for motorists – and that they are not going to give up an inch of space for bicyclists.

**Pedestrian facilities** are the third green infrastructure layer. A complete system of pedestrian sidewalks and crossings is perhaps the most basic and necessary element of a community's infrastructure. Sidewalks are the place where children and seniors travel, where neighbors meet, where urban business and culture take place. Unfortunately, again, America has forgotten to build this critical layer in many of our communities. American suburbia has been built on the assumption that the automobile will carry us to every destination. For decades, sidewalks were seen as a waste of valuable land by developers and as a maintenance headache by home owners and municipalities. Street crossings were generally an afterthought to engineers who designed for the automobile first, and in fact pedestrians were often considered "impedances" in the flow of motor traffic.

Like on-street bicycle facilities, the typical street elements for pedestrian mobility are inherently simple. Sidewalks are generally made from concrete with technology that dates back to the Romans. They are generally set back from the street by a landscaped space which also includes utilities and space for ramps and driveways. That's it: five feet of concrete, a few feet of grass, add some trees and homes with front porches, and you've created the American small town of Norman Rockwell. In larger cities, the sidewalks are wider to accommodate increased activity, and ground floor spaces need to connect with the pedestrian space of the street. Pedestrian crossings require careful attention to detail to make sure that drainage, handicap accessibility, visibility, signal timing and other features are done right.

It is the fine level of detail and small scale of pedestrian facilities that often makes them difficult to manage for many communities. A missing section of sidewalk, a signal that doesn't work, a clogged storm drain, worn-out pavement markings, snow and ice in winter can all make it impossible for people to walk. As a result, in many communities, pedestrians suffer the death of a thousand cuts – multiple small problems that combine to make walking unsafe, un-enjoyable and therefore unusable. Fixing these problems requires a focus on pedestrian scale issues.

Where most engineering manuals consider the huge tractor trailer truck as the typical 'design vehicle' for roadway design, here is another alternative: design streets so a grandmother can push a child in a stroller across the street. Imagine that it is your mother pushing your daughter in that stroller. Follow this advice on every street in your community and make improvements accordingly. Implement the systems and management practices to maintain these conditions. With this perspective on the scale of walking, your community will become a great place for pedestrians.

**Multimodal connections** are the final layer that makes non-motorized transportation work. Greenways, bicycle facilities and pedestrian infrastructure networks must be connected to motorized transportation systems. This makes it possible to travel longer distances. Bikes need to be carried on buses, trains, ferries and private cars. Pedestrians are the customers of transit, and transit needs to be designed and funded with this in mind. Simple details can make a significant difference in this layer, including: carefully designed bicycle parking at transit stations, pedestrian crossings at bus stops, accessible ramps, shade, benches and lighting that all create this human scaled environment. These interconnections between all modes of transportation (both motorized and non-motorized), are the keys to a functional green infrastructure.

The layer of multimodal connections requires agencies and organizations to re-think the concept of mobility at a basic level. The design of transit facilities and vehicles takes on a new perspective when pedestrians and bicyclists become part of the process. Making transit stops accessible for the disabled also makes it easier for bicyclists. Designing streetcar tracks so that bicyclists won't get their wheels caught in them also makes the street safer for pedestrians and motorists. Even putting bike racks on cars is part of this layer, since combining travel by bicycles and cars can reduce some fossil-fueled trips.

A more recent innovation is the development of urban bike sharing systems, which combine the flexibility of bicycling with the technology of wireless, solar-powered rental stations. This technology has been deployed in large scale systems in Paris, London, Montreal, Melbourne, Washington, Boston and other cities. The idea of bike sharing is a classic example of third mode thinking. It provides a new way to make short trips in urban areas in a niche that fits between walking and transit. You simply swipe a credit card and take a bicycle, ride it to the next station, and return the bike. As this technology evolves, it is quickly changing the way people travel and enjoy urban life. Our company has entered this market with a new business called Alta Bicycle Share, and we are managing fleets of urban bikes in Boston, New York and other cities. In Washington, D.C. the new Capital Bike Share ("CABI") system registered 1,000,000 trips in its first year.

By creating combinations of trips, the integration of bicycling, walking and transit has the potential to shift mobility from a monoculture of car driving to a multi-modal system of transportation choices. It is important to note that building all four layers of green mobility infrastructure is not enough to create a complete change in a community's transportation patterns. In addition to the built environment, a balanced program of education, encouragement, enforcement, and evaluation needs to be provided. These "E's" have formed the basis of the League of American Bicyclists innovative Bicycle Friendly Communities (BFC) initiative. The BFC process awards bronze, silver, gold and platinum status to communities that succeed in all of these areas.

The best award-winning communities, including Portland, Minneapolis, San Francisco and Denver have all shown that when green infrastructure is supported by programs to educate motorists, pedestrians and bicyclists about the rules of the road, when the public is encouraged to participate in a healthy lifestyle, when law enforcement protects public safety and these programs are routinely evaluated for performance benchmarks, then a truly complete green infrastructure is in place. What these cities all share in common is a built environment with a foundation of the four layers: greenways, on-street bikeways, pedestrian facilities and multi-modal connections. The best communities have the leadership and vision to make all four layers possible. They have made the third mode possible for their residents, visitors and businesses, and have made it possible for all of us to see a future that is greener and more sustainable.

# 4. THE NATIONAL PARKING LOT SERVICE

## Grand Canyon

Grand Canyon Vision:

> "...keep this great wonder of nature as it is now...keep it for your children, your children's children, and all who come after you, as the one great sight which every American...should see."

President Theodore Roosevelt

In 1997, a group of volunteers gathered at Grand Canyon National Park to plan and develop a Greenway system along the rim of the Canyon. The vision of the Grand Canyon Greenway was to transform one of the world's most important places from an automobile-dominated experience of driving their cars from one overlook to the next into a model for sustainability based on people bicycling, walking and using trails along the rim of the Canyon. The project was intended as a millennium gift for the United States to celebrate in the year 2000. It didn't quite turn out that way, and the story provides important lessons for creating third-mode solutions.

In October, 2010, the fifth phase of the Grand Canyon Greenway was opened to the public, 15 years after the project was proposed in the Park's General Management Plan. The final section of the first phase of the Greenway system is scheduled for construction in 2012. In many ways, the Grand Canyon Greenway answers the question: "What happens when you combine a team of leaders in a growing national movement, a world heritage site with an outdated infrastructure, and a nation challenged by issues of nature deficit disorder, a physical inactivity epidemic, and an addiction to fossil fuels?" This project, its ups and downs, challenges and opportunities, is a microcosm of the green infrastructure movement in America.

The team that assembled in 1997 was not the first to imagine a better way to visit our National Parks. In 1968, Edward Abbey published his classic book, "Desert Solitaire" which describes the concept for the Grand Canyon Greenway project as follows:

*"There is no compelling reason, for example, why tourists need to drive their automobiles to the very brink of the Grand Canyon's south rim. They could walk that last mile. Better yet, the Park Service should build an enormous parking lot about ten miles south of Grand Canyon Village and another east of Desert View. At those points, as at Yosemite, our people could emerge from their steaming shells of steel and glass and climb upon horses or bicycles for the final leg of the journey. On the rim, as at present, the hotels and restaurants will remain to serve the physical needs of the park visitors. Trips along the rim would also be made on foot, on horseback, or utilizing the paved road which already exists on bicycles. For those willing to go all the way from one parking lot to the other, a distance of some sixty or seventy miles, we might provide bus service back to their cars, a service which would at the same time effect a convenient exchange of bicycles*

*and/or horses between the two terminals."*
Abbey's vision for the National Parks was compelling, but it was not acted upon for decades. By the late 1980s Grand Canyon was dealing with more than 4.5 million visitors a year and their "steaming shells of steel and glass." Visitors were spending a lot of time stuck in traffic jams, and even after a five hour drive from Phoenix or Las Vegas, many were spending more time in the Park's gift shops than they were looking out at the Canyon. In 1990, I travelled with my wife, Margo, a former ranger at Grand Canyon, Sequoia and Kings Canyon, and toured the National Parks. It was the first time in my life that I had been west of the Mississippi, and the first time I saw the Grand Canyon. I had travelled up and down the East Coast, lived in Italy, toured through Europe and visited the Middle East before I saw most of my own country.

Thank God I married a former park ranger. Going out west in the summer of 1990 turned out to be a significant turning point in my life. We flew to Las Vegas, rented a white Mustang convertible, and began a 4,000 mile adventure through the Southwest. Our trip began with a one night stay with Margo's friends at the North Rim of the Grand Canyon. The next day, they took us on a rafting trip down the San Juan River from the Four Corners to the Colorado River. We were joined on the river by another friend and former ranger, who brought along her fiancé. That first 24 hours in the Southwest set in motion a series of events that are still hard to believe. I was instantly hooked by the beauty of the canyon country. The new couple, Marlene and Dar Crammond, convinced us to re-route our trip that summer to include a return visit to their wedding at Grand Canyon in early August. The river trip was incredible, and so were our travels through Bryce, Zion, Capital Reef, Mesa Verde, Arches,

Sequoia, Yosemite and Kings Canyon National Parks.

A month later, we were sitting at a beach near Monterey, California, debating whether or not we should drive 16 hours across California, Nevada and Utah to get to the wedding. We only had a week left before we were set to fly back home from Las Vegas. With one last push, we decided to drive up to Yosemite and across the desert back to the North Rim in time for the wedding. We camped at Toulumne Meadows and then left at dawn for a 16 hour road trip. We didn't quite make it all the way to our destination that day, and ended up north of Las Vegas looking for a place to stay. We stumbled upon a small hot springs resort on the Virgin River called Pah Tempe outside of Hurricane Utah that night. There was a full moon, and it was a magical place that I would return to several times on future trips. Sadly, the springs have since been closed in a local political battle that is tied to the ongoing water rights battles caused by the sprawling development of the Las Vegas region.

By the time we got to the wedding at Grand Canyon, I was completely amazed by the Colorado Plateau, but the best was yet to come. Several members of the wedding party were from Flagstaff, and they had brought new full suspension mountain bikes. These were the first modern mountain bikes that I had seen, but before I could ride one we were told by National Park Service staff that bicycles were officially banned from using trails in Grand Canyon. I was shocked by this and could not understand why riding a bicycle was not allowed – not just at Grand Canyon, but in most of the National Parks. I didn't want to ride down into the Canyon, I just wanted to bike along the rim, to the campground and to the visitor's center instead of driving a car. Making this simple idea possible turned out to be a bigger challenge than I realized.

At a campfire discussion that evening, I started asking our friends and some of the Park Service staff, "why can't we change this policy?" One of the guests around the fire was Park planner Brad Traver, who talked about Grand Canyon's upcoming general management plan, and how transportation was going to be a major issue. Brad suggested that I get on the Park's mailing list for the new plan. Many of the wedding guests clearly thought the bike ban should be overturned, and that the National Parks should be models for biking and walking instead of driving. Without realizing it at the time, the beginnings of a bold new project had started to take shape. That campfire conversation would lead to more than a decade of work towards turning the greenway vision into reality.

The wedding was a memorable event, with new friends, a full moon over the Canyon, and these new ideas in my head. One day, I took a ride with Dar out to an overlook called Point Sublime. It was an epic ride – and still one of the most amazing days I've ever had in the outdoors - but it took place outside the National Park boundary because bicycles were banned on the Park's trails. We rode through the National Forest lands parallel to the Canyon's rim for more than 20 miles that day. It was a lot of climbing and riding on rocky old jeep roads. We didn't see the Canyon for most of the ride.

As we came to the top of our last uphill section, I blew a tire on my bike. The tube was shredded and could not be patched. It turned out that the spare tube we had with us was for the wrong type of valve. The hole in the rim was too small for the new tube. To make matters worse, my bike was brand new, and belonged to our friend Dale Schmidt. Our wives were following us with a pickup truck full of smoked Colorado River trout and cold beer, but we didn't want to wait until they showed up. We finally decided that Dale would appreciate our self-sufficiency if we solved the problem ourselves. We augured out a larger hole in his brand-new rim with a Swiss Army knife, got the tire fixed, and finished the ride.

That last climb led to an incredible downhill. We crested a ridge and could feel the land drop away from us down towards the rim. Soon, we were flying downhill through the trees, accelerating with gravity as the view began to open up, and finally arriving out onto the knife edge of Point Sublime to one of the most amazing landscapes on Earth. I was exhausted, amazed and my breath was taken away by both the view and the high altitude. There is a memorable photo of that day with me sleeping in the middle of our picnic with a cold beer in my hand. After that ride, I couldn't help but start thinking of a way to make that experience of the Grand Canyon into something that the Park's millions of visitors could enjoy.

Five years later, in 1995, I received a copy of the new Grand Canyon General Management plan in the mail from the National Park Service. I had stayed on their mailing list since our trip out west. At that point, I was working as New York State DOT's bicycle and pedestrian program manager. I was developing bike, pedestrian and greenway projects through the new ISTEA federal transportation bill, which for the first time provided significant funding for active transportation. When I opened the Grand Canyon plan, I noticed that it included the idea of a greenway system for the Park, but there were no specifics on how or when it would be implemented. The plan's major emphasis appeared to be a new Heritage Education Campus and a light rail transit system along the South Rim - projects that I knew would cost far more than a network of trails. I thought that it was time to develop a new kind of project, a national model for the growing greenways movement: the Grand Canyon Greenway.

In early 1996, I wrote a simple letter to Robert Arnberger, Superintendent of Grand Canyon National Park. We had never met. The letter said that I wanted to assemble a volunteer team of national leaders from the growing Greenways movement to develop a pro-bono plan to create the Grand Canyon Greenway. I honestly had no idea if this was really possible, but it seemed like it was worth a try. Superintendent Arnberger asked his new General Management Plan Implementation Team Leader, Brad Traver (whom I had met around the North Rim camp fire back in 1990) to call me back, and he asked a few simple questions: Who are you? Are you serious? and, When can we meet? We agreed to meet in Las Vegas in April, where I had been asked by Walkable Communities guru Dan Burden to help lead a workshop on the redesign of the Las Vegas Strip.

Dan and I figured that if we could handle a project as complex as Vegas, then maybe anything was possible. Brad Traver met with us in the lobby of a Hampton Inn a few blocks off the Strip. He saw the level and quality of the work we were doing in Las Vegas, and he agreed that a similar workshop could be set up for the Grand Canyon Greenway. Brad also introduced us to Bob Koons, the President of the Grand Canyon National Park Foundation, which had been formed in 1995 to create public-private partnerships to support the Park. We convinced Bob that we knew a core group of people from throughout the U.S. who would volunteer for the project, if the Foundation would provide travel, expenses and support for a "Greenway Summit" workshop at Grand Canyon National Park.

Over the next few months, I very cautiously approached key people about the concept for the Grand Canyon Greenway, but I was still unsure if the plan would really work. I spoke with Mark Fenton, editor at Walking Magazine, at a meeting in Boulder, Colorado to test the idea. He instantly said, "count me in." I then called Chuck Flink of Greenways, Inc., and he said the same. So did Andy Clarke, then a Vice President with Rails-to-Trails Conservancy, and Charlie Gandy of the Bicycle Federation of America. With just a few requests to key people, the Greenway idea was starting to gain momentum. The initial group agreed that the September, 1996 Pro Walk/Pro Bike Conference in Portland, Maine would be a good place to meet and add key members to the team. Bob Koons joined us in Portland, and after a short announcement was made from the conference podium asking for people who wanted to be involved in a visionary project, our first meeting took place.

A key person who volunteered to join us at that meeting in Portland was Peter Axelson of Beneficial Designs. Peter is one of those rare individuals who inspires everyone he meets, and he is one of the nation's best designers of universally accessible trails. Peter is a great engineer, flies his own plane, and is a paraplegic. By the end of that first meeting, Bob Koons was convinced that the Grand Canyon Greenway was possible, and agreed to host the team for a Grand Canyon Greenway Summit in January, 2007. I was given the task of developing the framework, and Koons agreed to use funding from the new American Airlines "Miles for Trails" program to pay for the volunteers' travel and expenses.

Before the meeting was over, Chuck Flink offered a key piece of advice for the team: we need to get Bob Searns involved in the project. Bob and Chuck had co-authored the book "Greenways," and Bob was then president of the consulting firm Urban Edges in Denver. In one phone call, Searns immediately said the same thing the rest of the team had said, "say 'when' – this is a once in a lifetime opportunity." By January, 1997, the team of volunteers included myself, Chuck Flink, Bob Searns, Mark Fenton, Andy Clarke, Peter Axelson, Charlie Gandy, landscape architect Betty Drake of Arizona, State Bike / Pedestrian Coordinator Sue Newberry of Nevada, and engineer Ben Pugh of California.

We had established a working arrangement with the Grand Canyon Foundation and Brad Traver's new general management plan implementation team at the Park (including Landscape Architect Bob Pilk, communications specialist Mallory Smith, and planner Gigi Wright). The first Grand Canyon Greenway Summit was held over Super Bowl weekend in January, 1997 at the Albright Training Center on the South Rim. Chuck Flink led the design group, and Bob Searns led the development group, and I served as overall project leader. The National Park Service, Grand Canyon Foundation and the Greenway team volunteers worked more than 50 hours over the course of three intense days before presenting the concepts for a comprehensive greenway infrastructure and implementation strategy to Superintendent Arnberger.

With so much expertise on the team and a direct connection to decision makers, the creative energy was extraordinary. In one hour, Dan Burden sketched out an elegant solution for moving thousands of visitors around the Mather Point Visitors' Center. The development team came up with a concept for using revenue from the rental of bicycles, strollers, wheelchairs and daypacks as an ongoing endowment for trail maintenance. In the middle of the night before the presentation, Margo and came up with a concept for the Greenway as the 'trail of time' to interpret the geologic history of the Canyon along the South Rim. The next morning, Bob Pilk illustrated the concept and Chuck Flink used a digital camera to import the image into PowerPoint slides before the presentation began.

I still hadn't met the Superintendent when Brad took me to his office that Monday morning, a half hour before the presentation. We had been up most of the night preparing our graphics and an Action Plan to move the project forward. As Brad and I sat in an outer office, I could hear the Superintendent screaming over the phone at somebody. I was glad that I wasn't on the other end of that call. All I could think was that I was taking a huge risk with my career and the reputations of some of the top trails people in the world. I nervously introduced myself, and after just a few moments, the Superintendent said bluntly, "well then, let's go get started."

The presentation went like clockwork, with each team member sharing the work our volunteers had created. We had a detailed strategy for fundraising, and state-of-the-practice trail design. Brad had assembled a large group of key Park staff and Foundation representatives, but it was hard to tell if they were all on board with our ideas. Knowing that I was speaking last, I had taken a check from our personal checkbook and written out a donation to the Foundation as a way to express our team's gratitude for the opportunity. But, before I got my turn, Charlie Gandy ad-libbed his fundraising presentation, took out his own checkbook and made out a donation to the Foundation, too. Before the morning was over, our team donated more than $1,000 to a project that we had all volunteered for. By the time we were done, I knew that we had done everything possible to help turn our ideas for the Grand Canyon Greenway into reality.

The Superintendent, in turn, responded by delivering his own powerful response to close the Summit, calling the Greenway action plan 'the greatest gift given to the National Parks in his career,' and offering 'to do anything within his power to keep this team together to complete the Greenway.' If there was a defining moment in the story of the Grand Canyon Greenway, it was when Superintendent Arnberger spoke at the end of that first summit. His words were so deeply heartfelt, so direct, and so inspiring. The team's presentation moved the Superintendent to make the Greenway a priority project equal to the Heritage Education Campus and light rail transit initiatives.

Bear in mind that before he walked into the room that morning, none of us had ever met the Superintendent, and nobody had even suggested the idea of "keeping the team together." The volunteers had staked their reputations on a high risk adventure simply because they believed it was a rare opportunity. But before that day was over, the volunteers agreed to form a working group called The Greenways Collaborative (TGC), and to continue working on the project until it was built. We left the Canyon that week with a memorable phrase that the Superintendent liked to use for challenging situations: "Now we're in it."

As trail professionals, the opportunity to work on such a significant project was enough to motivate everyone involved. Imagine being able to hike along the rim with Mark Fenton (a former Olympic race walker and national health expert) or experience the built environment with Peter Axelson, who is a world leader in accessible design. During the first workshop, Andy Clarke identified an Arizona DOT request for ISTEA Transportation Enhancements funds, and co-authored a grant application that would lead to the first major funding for implementing the Greenway. The optimism of the Greenway Collaborative was extraordinary and there was a real sense that this project would get done as a Millennium gift to our nation. There was even an invitation sent to President Clinton, asking him to attend the groundbreaking on July 4th, 2000. We mailed it from the Grand Canyon post office and included a scanned copy in the Greenway plan.

As the project gained momentum, the Park Service and the Foundation provided incredible support for the team and the Greenway. The field work involved exploring potential trail corridors along the rim, creating connections to Park gateways, and focus group meetings with Park staff and visitors to understand the key issues. A highlight for the volunteers during the first Summit was a dinner hosted by the Foundation at the El Tovar Hotel. That dinner, some vintage bottles of red wine and the opportunity to experience one of the world's great wonders was more than enough to inspire the team

However, developing the Greenway was not destined to be a completely smooth process, in part because of competing interests, turf battles for control of the project, and differing visions for the future of our National Parks. A key part of this inherent conflict was the concept that two major projects would define the future of Grand Canyon National Park: the new light rail transit line along the South Rim and the proposed Heritage Education Campus to be built around the old power station near the El Tovar Hotel. These were big-ticket projects with costs estimated in the hundreds of millions of dollars. Controversy about 'banning cars from the Park' and the high cost of other solutions was a challenge that the Greenway system could help resolve. The Greenway was proposed as a realistic way to move some of the Park's more than 4.5 million annual visitors in a way that cost less, connected people with the natural environment and solved the paradox of how to improve Park access without limiting the visitor experience.

Superintendent Arnberger invited the team back to continue working on the Greenway plan. The second Grand Canyon Greenway Summit was held on the North Rim, over the July 4th weekend in 1997. The volunteers participated under the new umbrella of The Greenway Collaborative (TGC) and the team was asked to develop a new vision of the trails system for the North rim. In a memorable team building experience, we arranged for everyone to meet at the Pah Tempe Hot Springs in Hurricane for a two day retreat before the summit. The group arrived at the Park the following day well organized and ready for work. The North Rim is a remote destination, like an island in the sky, with a fraction of the visitors as at the South Rim and a more compact infrastructure. The team developed a concept for removing cars from in front of the historic Grand Canyon Lodge to create a pedestrian plaza, with a spine trail linking the hotel, visitor's center, and campground areas to the

North Kaibab trailhead.

In what would prove to be another key moment, a late night discussion about turning plans into action (following a July 4th barbeque hosted for the project by the Foundation) led to a set of traffic cones being placed across the road in front of the Lodge. The next morning, the former parking area was filled with people enjoying the space, taking pictures of the historic hotel, sharing a morning coffee and experiencing the Park's first new car-free plaza. This physical change was a simple but powerful demonstration that the ideas for the Greenway were good ideas. The cones were still there several years later, and it was only recently that the plaza has been re-designed as a permanent public space.

At the conclusion of the July workshop, the Foundation, NPS and TGC signed a historic Memorandum of Understanding (M.O.U.) at Grand Canyon Lodge to cooperatively implement the Grand Canyon Greenway – another first for all the organizations involved. Peter Axelson created an incredible memory for all in attendance at the signing ceremony on the patio overlooking Bright Angel Point. At the start of the event, Peter came down the stairs from the Lodge to the patio in his custom 'Cobra' wheelchair. The people on the patio cheered him on, and then called for an encore. Needless to say, Peter went back up to the top and did his entrance again, creating even louder applause – and another reminder that we are all working together to create universal access for people of all abilities. I then signed the M.O.U. agreement on behalf of the team, along with Rob Arnberger and Bob Koons – at the same place where our friends had been married on the North Rim of the Grand Canyon in 1990.

The Greenway Collaborative returned for a third time for a South

Rim Village Summit in January, 1998. This third volunteer-led workshop was arranged to develop the core Grand Canyon Village section of the Greenway through the Heritage Education Campus, campgrounds and lodging areas between the two proposed transit stations. Advocates from the Arizona Trail were involved to identify connections with their cross-state project, which included significant equestrian interest and statewide support. By the conclusion of this third workshop, the National Park Service estimated that the volunteers of the Greenway Collaborative had donated more than $250,000 in professional services for the Grand Canyon Greenway. The Park Service now had a detailed greenway plan, a fundraising strategy, grant applications for development, and positive momentum to move the project towards implementation.

In another unforgettable moment during the January, 1998 workshop, Bob Searns and I decided to conduct a field visit along an existing power line parallel to the South Rim. It was rough going as we traversed the rubble strewn corridor, but the alignment looked like a possible way to create a short term connection between Mather Point and the Arizona Trail for hiking, mountain biking and equestrian use. Bob was convinced that with a portable rock crusher and a good trails crew, the project could be implemented quickly. After a couple of hours, we decided to cut over to the rim to see if a good viewpoint was nearby. We sat down on the edge of the canyon, looked down and saw two enormous birds far down below us.

I asked Bob, "What kind of birds are so big that we see them from here? Is there any chance that they could be condors?" The California condor had only been recently re-introduced to the Colorado Plateau, and neither of us had ever seen one in the wild. Slowly, the huge birds began spiraling on the thermals up towards the rim. Bob got out a pair of binoculars and said, "if those aren't condors, they're still the biggest birds I've ever seen". From nearly a mile below, the birds flew right to where we were sitting. They flew to within ten feet – close enough to be a little scary – and for us to read the wing tags of two California condors, numbers 87 and 92. They circled us for more than half an hour. It is impossible to describe moments like this – they are so rare in life and yet so likely to happen with good people in great places.

There were many other significant events on the Grand Canyon project, including another mountain bike ride with a South Rim ranger who took several of us to see the extraordinary network of old fire roads and jeep tracks between the gateway village of Tusayan and the South Rim. We saw elk, deer, and a unique landscape just a few moments away from the crowded tourist areas. It seemed obvious that these trails could be an important link to get people to experience the full range of the Canyon environment. Unfortunately, when our group returned from that tour, we were informed that the ranger had broken protocol by showing the team these existing routes. Those old paths were scheduled for re-vegetation by the Park Service and US Forest Service. This potential opportunity was excluded from the Greenway plan and was an early indicator that the project would have some difficult days ahead.

The year 1998 represented a significant shift in involvement in the project on several levels. I was recruited to leave my job with NYSDOT and move to Washington, D.C. and serve as director of the United States Millennium Trails initiative. I knew that my involvement as the Grand Canyon Greenway team leader would be limited once I had started in D.C. During that period, the Grand Canyon Foundation was working to implement the initial phases of the Greenway project. The first Transportation Enhancements grant had been successful, and Arizona DOT would eventually award more than $800,000 to the project. In order to expedite the process, key members of the Greenway Collaborative were asked to provide professional consulting services. Chuck Flink led this effort, and Greenways, Inc. began working with the National Park Service on detailed designs for the system. Peter Axelson and Bob Searns were also involved in the design phase. There were multiple trips to the Canyon by this sub-group, including key sessions where critical issues of ADA compliance, environmental issues and fundraising strategies were developed.

Working within the framework of the July, 1997 M.O.U., the Greenway Collaborative, Grand Canyon Foundation and the National Park Service moved the project forward. During this process, the Grand Canyon Foundation hired Deborah Tuck as its new Executive Director, and she took responsibility for the Foundation's fundraising efforts, including the Greenway and the Heritage Education Campus. Meanwhile, back in Washington, a new opportunity presented itself through my involvement at USDOT. In November, 1998 the Grand Canyon Greenway project was awarded $896,800 in Public Lands Highways discretionary (PLH) funds from the US Department of Transportation as part of the Millennium Trails initiative. The funding was awarded for a "proof of concept" section of the Greenway linking Grand Canyon Village, the Heritage Education Center, the proposed light rail system and the village of Tusayan. The Grand Canyon Greenway now had nearly $2 million in funding and was gathering considerable momentum.

Design work continued, and on May 19, 1999 a groundbreaking event was held with First Lady Hillary Rodham Clinton. The event included a dedication of the Grand Canyon Greenway as one of the 1,000 Millennium Trail trails projects that would be part of the nation's legacy for the year 2000. Deborah Tuck of the Foundation, USDOT Deputy Secretary Gene Conti, Park Superintendent Rob Arnberger and Peter Axelson of the Greenway Collaborative joined the First Lady on the podium. Axelson's speech was emotional and powerful as he described the Grand Canyon as a place that he was previously unable to visit, and how the Greenway would open up the experience of a World Heritage Site to people of all ages and abilities. The First Lady posed for a photo with the Grand Canyon Greenway team that day, and everyone was inspired by the potential for this great project.

Unfortunately, the year 2000 brought a series of additional changes that would delay and potentially threaten the Grand Canyon Greenway project. Superintendent Arnberger left Grand Canyon for a new position in Alaska, and the 2000 election resulted in a change in presidents, Arizona politics and Park Service leadership. Joe Alston became superintendent of Grand Canyon National Park, and Bruce Babbitt was replaced as Secretary of the Interior by Gail Norton. Following these changes, the process for implementing the Greenway was slowed as overall Park Service budgets were reduced and the National Park Service continued to deal with an ongoing backlog of maintenance and basic repair projects. Instead of being completed as a Millennium project, the Greenway was beginning to look like a long-term effort.

By early 2001, construction was finally underway on Phase I of the Greenway, which extended the existing South Rim Trail (Grand Canyon Village to Yavapai Point) through Mather Point and out to Pipe Creek Vista. Interior Secretary Norton walked the new Phase 1 greenway with Park Superintendent Alston in 2001, but this was not a public event and the Greenway team was not informed about it until after the Secretary's visit. A year later, Phase 1 was completed and in June 2002, a National Trails Day dedication event celebrated the completion of the first new section of the Grand Canyon Greenway. The original volunteer team was invited to attend the event, and Superintendent Alston was joined on the podium by Native American leaders from Indigenous Community Enterprises (ICE) of Flagstaff, Arizona. Thanks to an initiative supported by the Foundation board, the benches along the trails were built from locally harvested timber by ICE, and it was a moving experience to hear tribal leaders describe how this was the first contract between the tribe and the U.S. government.

By this time, the Grand Canyon Foundation was becoming successful in securing significant private sector funding to match the initial federal grants. In fact, the Foundation had begun promoting the Greenway on their website and printed materials as a project comparable to the much larger Heritage Education Campus initiative. Private sources now included American Airlines Miles for Trails, Dr. Scholl Foundation, Bikes Belong Coalition, Home Depot, and the Richard Haiman National Park

Foundation. Then a major gift of $1,000,000 was received from the Nina Mason Pulliam Charitable Trust. On that sunny National Trails Day in 2002, it seemed that the Greenway was well on its way to completion.

The following day, Superintendent Alston issued a press release retracting his comments from the event, saying that he didn't mean to imply that the full Greenway system would be implemented, and that only the first few phases on the South Rim would be developed. The Greenway Collaborative and the Grand Canyon Foundation were stunned by this turn of events, but it was just the beginning of a long struggle to keep the project alive. It was never made clear to the other M.O.U. partners why the project began to meet such resistance. At some levels, it appeared that the Park Service was not comfortable with the public-private partnership process and wanted to control the project without involvement from the other partners. This was partially due to the changes in leadership, but also due to the fact the Greenway Collaborative members were 'outsiders' and that the Greenway itself was not a mainstream solution promoted from within the agency.

Greenway Phase II, which connects the park's primary visitor center to Grand Canyon Village, was completed in 2003, but there was very little progress on other sections of the Greenway system for the next several years. The project clearly suffered from not having a clear champion to fight through all the obstacles that can slow down new ideas. The frustration was typified by two visits of the Greenway Collaborative to advance the North Rim Phase IV Greenway from Bright Angel Point to the North Kaibab Trailhead. In August, 2003, I was asked to join a group including Chuck Flink, Peter Axelson, Bob Searns, staff from Greenways, Inc. and the National Park Service to field survey and develop the detailed design for the North Rim. This section was designed to follow the alignment of a water line corridor from the Grand Canyon Lodge through the campgrounds and rangers' residential areas. It was clearly stated and recorded in the meeting minutes that a detailed environmental review was not required because National Environmental Policy Act (NEPA) clearance had already been conducted as part of the previous utility project.

A year later, Chuck, Bob and I were asked by the Foundation to return in July for another work session on the North Rim. Greenways, Inc. staff had flagged the centerline of the alignment in the field and produced a full set of construction documents the previous year. The Phase IV Greenway had still not been started, even though funding was in place. When Chuck asked why the project was stalled, he was told by Park Service staff that the project needed NEPA approval. Chuck opened his laptop and showed everyone the email from the previous year stating that NEPA review was not required because the project was in a previously permitted corridor. This was a frustrating moment for the project team, but it was only one of many challenges that the project was to face in the next several years.

Despite the delays in implementation, the Grand Canyon Greenway received several national recognitions including the Department of Interior's 2002 National Accessibility Leadership Award (for creating the longest accessible trail in the National Park System), the 2002 American Society of Landscape Architects Merit Award, and the 2001 Harvey Bell Memorial Award from the Western Trail Builders Association. In 2004, I co-chaired a special session at the annual meeting of the Transportation Research Board on innovative transportation solutions in the National Parks, and Chuck Flink provided a panel presentation about the Grand Canyon Greenway. Also in 2004, a second $1,000,000 private gift was donated to the project by the Ethel and Kemper Marley Foundation. Then, in 2005, $2,560,000 for the Greenway was earmarked in the reauthorization of the federal SAFETEA transportation bill by Arizona's Congressional delegation, bringing the total amount of funding for the project to $7,435,000. But despite the best efforts and these important successes, the process of getting the Greenway on the ground was still slow. At several points, I was reminded of Rob Arnberger's advice early in the project. While sitting along the rim, Rob pointed out into the Canyon and said, "just look at the geology here – that is the pace of change at the Grand Canyon."

Meanwhile, it became more difficult to keep the project team together as people moved on to new phases of their lives and the Park Service lost its institutional memory of the project. Brad Traver left the General Management Plan Implementation Team for a new position and it became clear that without his leadership the project would have a difficult time moving forward. At the same time, other people took ideas from the original plan. For example, the 'trail of time' illustrated in the original 1997 concept plan was used by a research team at a western university to apply for and receive federal grant funding to develop an interpretative exhibit for the Canyon's Rim. The Greenway Collaborative tried to communicate with this group but was never included in the process. At the same time, the National Park Service began doing more of the design work in-house, with Landscape Architect Michael Terzich in a lead role. The Foundation continued to try to control the flow of project funding from grants that they had received, but relationships between the Park Service and the Foundation were strained at best during this period.

By 2007, the only Greenway section that was in progress was the Hermit's Rest Road section, where the trail was integrated into a roadway reconstruction project. The vision of a fully connected system of more than 70 miles of greenways throughout the Park was a distant dream at best. The first 10 miles of greenway had taken more than a decade to complete. Even with funding in place and the majority of the design documents completed, there was little good news. It is important to note that this status was not limited to the Grand Canyon Greenway during this period. The National Park Service was struggling with an underfunded, outdated infrastructure and a visitor population that exceeded available staffing and resources. Housing for Park staff, basic maintenance and operations costs were seen as more significant needs. At the same time, these issues were the kinds of problems that the Greenway system could help the Park address – if a non-traditional solution could keep from getting lost in the traditional approaches to solving these kinds of problems.

In the spring of 2007, the Grand Canyon Foundation asked the Greenway Collaborative to produce a report on the status of Greenways in National Parks. I authored the report, which was entitled, "On the Right Path: Greenways and America's National Parks." It showed that there were very few successful examples of new greenways being built in the National Parks at that time.

In spite of the fact that greenways had become a major feature of many American cities during the 1990s (including the development of the Greenway System in New York City, Denver's Urban Greenway network, and the 400 mile San Francisco Bay Trail), the National Parks were not following this trend. The report showed that the Grand Canyon Greenway was among a handful of new greenway projects in the National Parks, although building a few miles of trail in nearly a decade was far less than what the original Grand Canyon Greenway Action Plan had envisioned.

The relationship between the Foundation and the National Park Service continued to deteriorate, and in the spring of 2008 I got a call from Deborah Tuck saying that she was resigning. The Grand Canyon National Park Foundation was "going out of business." Deborah told me that the Greenway project was "dead" and the funding would have to be returned to the donors. This was a crushing moment for a project that had been developed from generosity, optimism and hope for a better future. All of those years of effort, a great plan developed by the best planners and designers in the nation – and now the project had been stopped by forces beyond our control. There is no way to describe my reaction to that call. It was a career low point for me and for the whole team that had tried so hard to make this project happen. There was nothing that could be done about it.

A short time later, in the summer of 2008, I took my family on a classic tour of the Grand Circle of National Parks in Arizona and Utah. With Margo and our three kids (ages 8, 11 and 14) it was a great month of hiking and camping at Bryce, Zion, Capital Reef, Arches and across the Southwest. In a way, it was a new version of the first trip Margo and I had taken in 1990. When we reached the Grand Canyon, we set up camp on the North Rim and walked along the Transept Trail to my favorite restaurant in the world, the Grand Canyon Lodge. It was the same walk that Margo and I had taken on our first trip to the Canyon. It was the same place where our friends wedding was held, the same place where I'd signed that M.O.U. a decade before. After a beautiful dinner, we watched the sun set over the rim and I tried to tell my family how disappointed I was to return to the Park after so many years of effort – fully aware that the Greenway project had failed.

We started walking back in the twilight towards the North Rim campground, along the route of the proposed greenway. A few moments later, we came to clearing full of construction equipment, piles of stone and a newly graded path that looked exactly like the design drawings for the Greenway. The project was under construction. It was unbelievable, there alone in the late evening, to find that the Grand Canyon Greenway had somehow come back to life. In a moment, I had gone from huge disappointment to an indescribable feeling of success.

We walked back to the campground in the growing darkness along the roughly graded new Phase IV North Rim Greenway from Grand Canyon Lodge to the campground. On the way we were passed by two Asian women on bicycles who stopped to ask, "when will this trail be finished? We need bike trails here at the Grand Canyon." It was a surreal moment, and there was no way to answer their question that night. Had the project really returned from certain death? How could this have happened? Later that evening, our kids returned from the ranger's campfire program and said, "Dad, the ranger talked about how Grand Canyon is building new greenways to help the environment." Apparently, the project was very much alive.

The next morning, I went down to the Grand Canyon Lodge and found Maureen Oltrogge, a Park information officer who was one of the few staff who was still around from the time of the original Greenway workshops. She said that a new Superintendent, Steve Martin, had come to the Park from Yellowstone. He had heard about the Greenway project, and thought it was an important initiative. Superintendent Martin had resurrected the Greenway plans, found a way to keep the funding from being returned to the donors, and was moving forward to complete the Greenway system on both the North and South Rims. The North Rim gas station had even been converted to a bike rental shop, and there was also a new bike rental operation at Mather Point on the South Rim. It is unlikely that any project could go through more ups and downs on the way to completion.

I guess Yogi Berra was right – it really never is over until it's over. Phase IV of the Grand Canyon Greenway, which connects Bright Angel Point to the North Kaibab Trailhead on the North Rim was completed in 2009. A media release from the Park said that this segment of the Greenway marked the first time that park staff completed the design work and construction oversight in-house – although the alignment had been field surveyed and design documents completed by the Greenway Collaborative several years before. Phase V on the South Rim opened to the public in October, 2010, and the next phase to connect from the

Park entrance at Tusayan to the South Rim is currently in development. It has taken more than 15 years, three Presidents and four Park Superintendents to build the original "proof of concept" phase of the Grand Canyon Greenway.

So what can be learned from this project beyond some good stories? In the 20th century, Grand Canyon and many of our other signature National Parks had been developed with access provided primarily for two modes of travel: roads that were designed to take people in cars from one scenic view to another, and backcountry hiking trails that were not designed for bicycling, wheelchairs, or a wide variety of trail uses. As a result, the modern National Parks are oriented to one mode of travel: driving a private car. To some extent, the National Parks Service has tried to counter the overuse of automobiles with another single mode solution: mass transit. That is why a light rail line was proposed for the Grand Canyon – even if it was expensive and impractical. In order to really change these conditions, the National Park Service has to be willing to see that there are new "third mode" ways to solve these problems and provide a new model for both transportation and recreation.

For years, the paradox of how to accommodate more visitors without degrading the Parks could not be solved because the visitors were assumed to be visiting by motor vehicle. A more complete view of the problem would show that besides roads and transit, there is a third mode of park mobility: human power. By designing our parks based on human powered mobility, we have a real chance to connect people with nature. If the leadership at Grand Canyon National Park had fully believed in this vision 15 years ago, the problem would have already been solved. The next generation is ready and waiting for these solutions. As the National Parks Service moves towards its 100th anniversary in the year 2016, we can only hope that the third mode will be a significant part of the vision for America's National Parks in the future.

# 5. TRAFFIC CALMING

## Creating a Positive Process

Early in my work at the New York State Department of Transportation (NYSDOT), I learned the challenges of creating change within a large bureaucracy. In fact, on my first day in my new office, my first phone call turned out to be a major challenge. I had walked into my cubicle that day to find nothing but an empty desk, a telephone and a media release announcing my appointment as the state's first full time Bicycle and Pedestrian Program Manager. That first call came from Bob Ronayne, the director of the Route 9A Reconstruction Project – the state's name for the replacement of the West Side Highway in Manhattan. Bob, who I had never met, barked into the phone that he needed me to come up to his office immediately.

When I got up to the Route 9A office, I sat in a conference room and waited. Ronayne came in and wasted no time on introductions. "You're the new bike guy. Tell me how wide to make the bike path on the west side of Manhattan. We've had people working on this for a year and I need an answer this week." I told him that we could work it out right then, and quickly estimated that more than a million people were within 10 blocks of the path, which could mean tens of thousands of people using the path each day. I asked him how much space he had, and to simply make the path as wide as possible. We've got 10 feet for the bike path, and we can separate out the pedestrians, he said. I told him the path wasn't wide enough.

Eventually we reached a compromise with 50-75 feet of pedestrian esplanade, and a 16 foot bikeway. I also tried unsuccessfully to also get a bike lane included on the northbound side of the roadway. That was important since big city blocks like the Javits Convention Center would require bicyclists to either use the sidewalk or have to cross the busy Route 9A to get to and from the path along the river, even if they were just going uptown a few blocks. While not all of the recommendations were followed, I learned at that first meeting that there was at least some potential for making change at NYSDOT.

I had arrived at my job at NYSDOT in an indirect way. I was a New York State registered architect, had run my own small firm, and had co-founded a non-profit smart growth planning organization called the Saratoga Open Space Project while I was earning my master's degree in Public Policy. I had been encouraged to apply for the new NYSDOT bike job by people from two other state agencies who were involved with the Open Space Project. They had heard about the new 1991 federal transportation legislation called "ISTEA" and knew that the state was required by the feds to hire a new bike coordinator. They thought I'd be a good person for the job, but I was skeptical that an outsider would get hired. I had never worked for a government agency before.

My contacts at New York State Parks and the New York State Department of Environmental Conservation introduced me to a new organization called the New York Bicycling Coalition (NYBC). They hosted monthly meetings of a group called the "Chain Gang" at a pub across the street from NYSDOT's headquarters in Albany. I went one evening and found out that NYBC had already been lobbying for another candidate to fill the bike coordinator position. At that point, most of the other states had already hired their state coordinators. New York would eventually be the 49th state to do so, followed only by Vermont. In any case, I was still encouraged to apply, and was offered an interview. I thought that the interview was just a formality so the state could say they looked at a candidate from the private sector, but I was told to take the process seriously and eventually was offered the new job in the spring of 1992. It then took the state more than a year to get all the approvals in place through the civil service system, and I finally went to work in the winter of 1993.

I was fortunate to have a great mentor, Louis Rossi, who was the director of the NYSDOT Planning Division. Lou taught me more about how big agencies work and how to create change than anyone I'd met before. We had great leadership above us, including Commissioner John Egan, who was the kind of person you'd walk through fire for. I remember the first November after he took over at NYSDOT, because on Thanksgiving he sent a memo to the entire staff inviting anyone who needed a place for the holiday to come to his house for dinner. This was a real paper memo, delivered to everyone's desk with his home phone number on it. Two people took him up on the offer – one was from another country and had never been to American Thanksgiving. With leaders like that, I knew that we could make some big changes happen.

To test our limits, Lou Rossi asked me to develop a short list of high-profile projects that could be implemented quickly. We knew that New York City would be a top priority, along with the first Statewide Pedestrian/Bicycle Master Plan, and new design manuals for our agency. We also needed a statewide project, and came up with the idea of creating a network of signed on-road bike routes across New York State. We used the state's video inventory of the roadway system and figured that we could identify roads with good paved shoulders and link them up across the state. Lou asked me to develop a briefing for the Commissioner to get approval for the project. It was at that time that I learned a major lesson about leadership.

I arrived at Lou's office for the briefing as well prepared as I thought I could be. I clearly presented three alternatives for him and our key staff. This was something I had learned in architecture school – to develop at least three different options for any problem. Unfortunately, that was definitely not what Lou wanted, and he was clearly disappointed with the presentation. "What's wrong with these alternatives?" I asked. I'll never forget his reply. "Nothing," he said. "But what I want from you is solutions, not options. Go back to your office and develop a clear recommendation for us to take to the Commissioner. That is my job if you do yours. We hired you to be our expert, not to make your decisions for you. As long as the Governor signs your paycheck, your job is do your work better than anyone else knows how to do it."

That was a difficult but critical lesson for me to grasp. My boss was telling me, in no uncertain terms, that I had the latitude to do what I thought was best, and that he would back me up on my recommendations. The quality of my work had to be the best, done right and done right the first time. If I did my job well, then the leadership above me would provide resources and support. Once I followed that advice, I had the ability to move many of our projects forward and learned to "ask first and seek forgiveness later." That strategy was critical for making change happen in a huge agency.

For example, when we needed to get a letter sent out from the Commissioner to host a meeting of a new Statewide Bike/Pedestrian Advisory Council, I simply drafted the letter, told Lou what I was doing, and walked it upstairs for signature. When that same letter hadn't been signed for a few weeks, my staff tracked it down and got it signed. One particular Deputy Commissioner got bent out of shape over this, and called Lou and me into his office for a long screaming session. When I tried to defend my actions (the advisory committee meeting was scheduled for that week and the letter was really a formality) Lou simply handed me a note that said, "the protocols are secret and we will always be to blame." I knew what he meant, accepted my slap on the wrist from the Deputy, and we kept changing the agency, one day at a time.

I was lucky to find the spark of other key leaders while I worked for NYSDOT. Our transit division director, Lee Sander, held brown bag lunches to show Tom Peters management videos about change. Those sessions were probably over the heads of a lot of mainstream bureaucrats, but it helped to know that others were trying to change the system, too. For example, our chief construction engineer for the Route 9A project in Manhattan labeled the first phase of the new Greenway along the West Side as the "interim construction staging area." This made it possible to build the first mile of a new bike path from the World Trade Center up to Greenwich Village using funding from the West Side Highway – the staging area was 16 feet wide and a mile long, and just happened to be the same dimensions as the path.

One of our priority actions was to develop policies and guidelines for traffic calming in New York State. Traffic calming is a term used to describe techniques for creating streets where motor vehicles move more slowly, and where pedestrians and bicyclists have the ability to safely 'share the road.' The term became popular in the transportation profession in the 1990's as communities looked for third mode solutions without having to build separated facilities for each mode of travel. Traffic calming allowed creative designers and communities to change the dynamics of transportation by re-thinking the basic reasons for mobility.

As it turns out, the New York State Vehicle and Traffic Law, Section 152, defines "traffic" as, "Pedestrians...vehicles, bicycles, and other conveyances either singly or together while using any highway for the purposes of travel." This means that any traffic study, traffic engineering, or traffic planning and design should, by definition, be addressing the needs of all forms of traffic – including pedestrians and bicyclists. Needless to say, this was not the case at NYSDOT in the 1990's, but it was at least a starting point for trying to shift the engineering culture into some new third mode thinking.

A simple but effective example of traffic calming as a third mode solution is the modern roundabout. Circular intersections have primarily been used in the U.S. for large traffic circles like the rotaries in New England, but these were not always popular with the general public. Smaller scale 'modern roundabouts' become popular internationally, but the U.S. typically used conventional rectangular intersection controls such as stop signs and traffic signals. The biggest difference between the two types is that in a circular intersection, traffic never stops moving. In a rectangular intersection, half the traffic is usually stopped at any given time. If you can change intersections from rectangular to circular, then it is logical to believe that more traffic can move more efficiently. This change can help motorists, pedestrians and bicyclists by calming traffic for all modes of travel.

Unfortunately, the U.S. had limited experience with modern roundabouts. Cheap electricity, advances in traffic signal technology and the unfavorable experiences with larger multi-lane rotaries had created a preference for rectangular intersections. However, the modern roundabout offered a simple way to replace costly traffic signals and ineffective 4-way stop signs with a solution that worked better and costs less to maintain. In many cases, the modern roundabout provided improved safety, better access for pedestrians and bicyclists, and an opportunity to improve the streetscape visually. Needless to say, it took the transportation profession years to adopt this new way of seeing how intersections could work.

The rectangular intersection was ingrained in design manuals and professional practice but roundabouts were new. There were fears that emergency vehicles would be slowed down by them. Big trucks wouldn't be able to maneuver around them.

Snowplows would hit them. The list of excuses was endless and the resistance to change continued in spite of positive evidence. Seattle did a major installation of neighborhood roundabouts in the early 1990s that showed a clearly positive improvement over rectangular intersection treatments. Even historical examples from throughout the Northeast didn't help – there had been a time in the late 1800's when monuments were commonly placed in the center of intersections. One of my personal favorites is the circular fountain with a statue of a bear holding a streetlamp in the middle of Main Street in Geneseo, New York. That roundabout has been in place for more than a century and the bear is still standing.

Eventually, modern roundabouts and other traffic calming features became popular in American communities because they are simple solutions to complex problems. Roundabouts save energy, provide opportunities for public gardens and art, slow down motorized traffic, and make streets safer for pedestrians and bicyclists. People grow to like them, and they work better than conventional rectangular intersections. The round intersection moves traffic more efficiently, at lower cost and with less energy. That is an ideal third mode solution.

The implementation of traffic calming is a story about change, bureaucracy and the future of pedestrians in the American transportation system. Roundabouts were just one of dozens of new treatments that were not in the engineering manuals of the 1990s, and changing those manuals was seen as changing the very foundations of the traffic engineering profession. Let me say that I have always been a team player in the organizations I have worked for, and that this next story is being told honestly and openly in order to learn from it. I do not use individual names for obvious reasons, but I will describe what it took to establish a simple 'yield to pedestrians' traffic calming device in New York State. This is a good example of what it takes to overcome long-term institutional opposition to third mode thinking.

In 1993, the New York State Manual of Uniform Traffic Control Devices (MUTCD) did not include a sign which said "Yield to Pedestrians." It did, however, include signs to warn motorists about Amish horse drawn carriages, deer crossings, and how to find the nearest gas, food and lodgings from the freeway. Tragically, at that time approximately 300 pedestrians were being killed in New York State in a typical year. The fact that almost every single day a person is run over by another person driving a car (and that both are victims) had never led to the creation of a sign or device which communicated the State's pedestrian right of way law.

As the Bicycle and Pedestrian Program Manager at the New York State Department of Transportation, our top priority pedestrian initiative was to provide new crosswalks and pedestrian crossing signs in the 180 Central Business Districts which had 'Main Streets' on State numbered highways. This was much easier said than done. In spite of the fact that these *business* districts contribute substantially to the state's economy, pedestrians (a.k.a: "customers") had received very little attention in terms of infrastructure improvements. In fact, the term "Main Street" wasn't even mentioned in any of the New York State or federal transportation legislation of the 1990's. The relatively simple idea of creating signs which said "yield to pedestrians" and placing these signs in the crosswalk in the middle of the street had consistently met with significant resistance - in spite of support in many local communities.

In 1993, the reasons given for not communicating the need for motorists to yield to pedestrians were so numerous that they could be said to be cultural, not rational. NYSDOT's lawyers would say "you can't put a fixed object in the road." The engineers would say, "The text of the State law won't fit on a traffic sign." Maintenance crews would say, "Why do we need to do this in the first place?" This is the same kind of reasoning which has led many transportation professionals to believe that crosswalks are 'unsafe' and create a "false sense of security" for pedestrians - but that is another story.

The National Committee on Uniform Traffic Control Devices, which develops changes to the Federal MUTCD, had declined to standardize 'yield to pedestrians' signs, saying that it was a 'regional' issue. NYSDOT and other agencies from throughout New England had, for many years, prohibited local communities from installing devices which had messages like, "Give Pedestrians a Brake" or "Stop for Pedestrians." The rationale that these safety features were "not in the manual" served as a catch-all for not solving the problem - and for not seeing pedestrians as part of the traffic safety solution. Although local communities often solved the problem by making up their own signs and devices, none of the state engineers had provided a device that was approved for them to use.

In February of 1996, after a new political administration had taken office in New York State, a NYSDOT Traffic Calming

Task Force was established to resolve the 'yield to pedestrians' sign problem along with several other issues, and was given six months in which to report back to the Commissioner. This action was taken in part because New Jersey DOT had just lost a State Supreme Court case which ruled in favor of a town which had installed 'yield to pedestrians' devices, despite the lack of existing guidelines for them. NYSDOT leadership had started to realize that pro-actively resolving this issue in New York would show a more 'customer friendly' response for the new administration, and hopefully avoid the animosity experienced in New Jersey. Two events that occurred while the Task Force was developing its recommendations made this point clear.

In September of 1996, an 11 year old girl from upstate New York wrote to the Governor complaining that NYSDOT had removed the existing yield to pedestrians sign from a crosswalk in her town. The local newspaper, whose offices were located on Main Street at the same crosswalk, ran a photo showing a state trooper removing the sign, and noted that NYSDOT had ordered the removal. This was not the great public relations moment that New York State was working towards. NYSDOT, instead of being able to say, "Here are the guidelines for the type of sign you'd like to install," was instead forced to justify removing the signs because there were no guidelines – the signs were "not in the manual." In the second case, a downstate legislator on Long Island was so frustrated with NYSDOT's resistance to putting in "yield to pedestrians" devices in his town that he drafted a bill to take away NYSDOT's power to enforce the MUTCD in local communities. The bill passed both houses of the Legislature by a landslide. At one point, the legislator is said to have rolled up a copy of the bill inside a traffic cone and jammed the cone inside the NYSDOT Commissioner's front door. Now that's advocacy.

NYSDOT successfully argued that the bill restricting enforcement of the MUTCD could prohibit consistency of all traffic control devices (we still want all stop signs and traffic lights to look the same, don't we?) and it was vetoed by the Governor in October, 1996 - on the condition that NYSDOT finally develop "yield to pedestrians" signs. The NYSDOT Commissioner was asked to visit the legislator who had sponsored the bill and take a walk down his Main Street to resolve the issue. The Commissioner, the local mayor and others agreed that the new signs were a good idea. During their short walk, the consensus was that this seemed like a simple problem that could be resolved immediately, and that the matter had simply gotten out of hand. The Commissioner returned to Albany, and directed his staff to provide a solution to the problem. End of the story, right?

Wrong. It took more than a year after the Governor's veto message for the first new signs to be installed. As it turns out, the process of changing the MUTCD (and the system which enforces it) was even more byzantine than anyone could have possibly imagined. First there were a series of meetings with the Task Force, legal staff, and the Governor's Traffic Safety Committee, at which two basic issues were debated: 1) what should the sign say and 2) could any device be placed in the roadway? There was a strong sentiment that the State traffic law would have to be changed before a sign could be created. After much discussion, a national review of the differences in right-of-way laws and signage types, and more opinions than there were people involved, a sign graphic was finally developed. It simply said "Yield to Pedestrians in Crosswalk" and used a standard graphic of a pedestrian in a crosswalk instead of spelling out the full text. This met the requirements of New York State law, and allowed the sign to be created without new legislation. We finally had a sign which could be placed on a post on the side of the road. But that only solved half of the problem.

Local communities definitely wanted not just a sign, but a device that could be placed *in* the roadway at the center of the crosswalk, where motorists would clearly see it. To most traffic engineers, this was a "DFO," or deadly fixed object. To them, this was absolutely not allowed. These were the same people who referred to pedestrians as "impedance to traffic flow," in spite of the fact that the legal definition of "traffic" includes pedestrians and bicyclists. To local communities, including the 11-year old who wrote to the Governor and the Mayor from Long Island, the devices were a necessary way to slow down motorists so people could cross the street. To be fair to the engineers, many communities had installed devices which had messages other than the state law, on metal posts with hardware which could potentially go flying through the air and injure someone. As one elected official said, "If that's the problem, why don't we make these things out of rubber?" That turned out to be a significant comment.

The problem of solving how to produce the crosswalk devices came down to a single exchange at a key Task Force meeting. The question I asked was: "Why don't we make these things the same way we make devices to protect construction workers on our highway projects? If we can use devices to protect our employees while cars are going by at 65 mph, why can't we make a device to protect people on Main Street where cars are going 25 mph?" This line of reasoning finally broke the ice. Once we agreed to design something which was based on the same principles as our 'regular' highway devices, the solution was simple. We could make the pedestrian devices out of orange traffic cones, reflective mesh and plastic tubing.

Using manufacturers' catalogs for traffic safety products, NYSDOT engineers developed detailed specifications for a Supplementary Pedestrian Crossing Channelization Device (SPCCD). Similar materials had been crash-tested by the New Jersey State Police, and vendors were ready to supply them out of stock assemblies. The device would be made of traffic cone rubber and fitted with a safety orange, reflective fabric 'jacket' bearing the state law message, at a cost of about $150 each. The details were submitted for inclusion in the NYS MUTCD in December, 1996. Done deal, right?

Wrong again. If only the story had ended at this point. The clearance process to get the signs and devices into the MUTCD lasted until April 1997. Of even greater concern, internal opposition within NYSDOT to actually install the devices continued to stall implementation. In spite of the fact that by this time a federal funding source had been identified to install and field test the devices, agency staff continued to delay action on the Governor's October 1996 veto message. Consciously or unconsciously, some people simply did not want to do this. Every possible obstacle to maintain control and limit use of the devices was created. Requirements were added to the specifications mandating that a state highway work permit be issued for each device. Local communities were required to purchase, install and maintain the SPCCD's, without State funding. Finally, a waiver was required to be signed by the local community assuming liability if any of the devices were provided by NYSDOT for local use. Replacing existing non-conforming devices was the responsibility of the local community, and would not be offered as part of a statewide program.

We found funding to allow distribution of the devices in a limited test sample of 40 units, which my staff purchased for display at the New York State Bicycle and Pedestrian Conference in May, 1997. As of the summer of 1997 progressed, a handful of highway work permits had finally been issued, the signs and SPCCD's were finally in the MUTCD, and a field testing program was underway with help from the Federal Highway Administration, the University of North Carolina Highway Research Center, and Rensselaer Polytechnic Institute. However, the original idea of deploying new crosswalks and pedestrian safety signs on the Main Streets of the 180 central business districts in New York State was still far from reality.

New York, New Jersey and a few other states were innovators on this issue, but it was not until the federal MUTCD finally included standardized designs for "Yield to Pedestrians" signage that these devices finally started to be used throughout the United States. By that time, several states had gone through the long process of developing similar solutions. My wife has said that I should use one of the "Yield to Pedestrians" traffic cones as my gravestone. I know that more than a few engineers have had the same idea. It took more than a decade of effort to get them "in the manual" and even that was not enough to change the traffic engineering mindset. A simple device, one of dozens of necessary traffic calming features, should not take a decade to develop. There are many other changes that need to be made to make lower speeds and more balanced traffic a typical experience on the streets of America.

What third mode lessons can be learned from this experience?

1. **The Customer Is Always Right – If You Know Who The Customer Is:**

   What local communities wanted to do in this case was to serve their pedestrian customers. The resistance to standardizing the "Yield to Pedestrians" devices only resulted in dozens of different designs which were confusing to both motorists and pedestrians. Attempts to control "illegal" sign use by regulatory enforcement was a failure - and the lack of official guidelines only aggravated the problem. The traffic engineers had forgotten who their customers were.

2. **Just Say "YES"**

   The engineers' rationale that the "Yield to Pedestrians" signs were "not in the manual" was often met with people saying "then why don't you change the manual?" In spite of the way it is often used, the MUTCD was not written by Moses on the mountain. It is a guideline, not a standard. Instead of always saying "no" to what communities said they needed, the engineers involved in this process had to learn to say yes - and to turn a negative situation into a positive 'win-win' outcome.

3. **Lead, Follow or Get Out of the Way!**

   Learning to capitalize on an opportunity is a critical lesson in leadership. The fact that communities were taking the initiative to put up 'yield to pedestrians' signs in response to their perceptions of public safety was a good thing in itself. NYSDOT had the opportunity to simply standardize this process, and to look good in doing so, long before the Governor's directive. This was a missed opportunity to be leaders – and good organizations know how to capitalize on that kind of opportunity.

As challenging as the NYDOT's efforts were in the 1990's, they were still years ahead of most of the nation trying to resolve the "simple" issue of communicating the pedestrian right of way laws. Eventually, we got the roundabouts, "yield to pedestrians" devices and a variety of other traffic calming features approved in their own chapter of the State Highway Design Manual. I hope those efforts made it easier for others to move this issue forward, but we still have a long way to go. Pedestrian safety is a global issue, and traffic calming is still far from mainstream practice in traffic engineering. We owe our thanks to the many people who are working hard - often against great odds- to make these efforts possible. The honest telling of this "inside" story should serve as a real lesson in third mode leadership.

This is what it takes to make change happen in a bureaucracy. This is what it takes to make pedestrians, bicyclists, and third mode thinking part of the American transportation system. Everyone, from the Governor of New York State to an 11 year-old girl, is part of the process. Traffic engineers, planners, lawyers, elected officials and citizens have played a key role both by defining the opposition to progress and, for the best of the transportation profession, recognizing the need for change and stepping forward to make it happen. What have I learned? As John Fegan, the former USDOT Bicycle and Pedestrian Program

Manager often said, "be assertive - not aggressive." If ever patience was a virtue, then this is the right business to be in. Someday, every crosswalk will be well marked and include a device which says "Yield to Pedestrians." And every traffic engineer will design every street so it's safe for his mother to push his child in a stroller. Then we will know that the third mode has become part of the mainstream.

# 6. COMPLETE STREETS

## The Integration of Transportation

Around the world, extraordinary efforts are being made by progressive communities to reinvent their infrastructure. Few moments sum up these efforts more than an incredible event that took place on July 18, 2010, when the Autobahn A40 near Essen, Germany was 'car-less' on a Sunday afternoon and more than 3 million people celebrated a cultural event on the famous highway. People walked and cycled along the Autobahn, and 20,000 picnic tables were lined up end-to-end after the road was cleared of its usual motorized traffic. The 40-mile-long stretch of one of Europe's busiest motorways, between the cities of Dortmund and Duisburg, became a stream of pedestrians and cyclists. As reported by the Christian Science Monitor, "cars were strictly verboten." It is hard to imagine a similar event taking place in the U.S. What if I-95 on the east coast between Washington DC and Baltimore was used by people instead of motor vehicles for a day? Germany, as one of the leading 'green' innovators in the world, proved that such an impossible idea was possible – and successful.

Not all communities can accomplish an event on the scale of what Dortmund created, but the underlying concept is important globally: our infrastructure is public space that can be used in innovative ways. The one-size-fits-all mentality of our mono-modal motorized society doesn't have to be the only alternative. In New York City, the New York Marathon, the 5 Boro Bike Tour, street festivals and major parades frequently allow people to take over major roads as public space, and cities from Portland to Paris are creating similar opportunities. Portland's annual "Bridge Pedal" is a defining event for the city, as tens of thousands of bicyclists enjoy a car-free day. Paris opens the road along the Seine each summer as a public esplanade, complete with temporary sand beaches and floating swimming pools on barges.

Many cities are following the lead of Bogota, Columbia, which led a movement of "Ciclovias" where major roads were opened up to people every week. While initially promoted as a way to reduce air pollution, the events quickly became a social movement. Bogota's innovative leadership team of Mayor Enrique Penalosa and his brother, Public Works Director Gil Penalosa, realized the power of human powered transportation. In a city of more than 6 million people, the Penalosa brothers knew that the majority of infrastructure funding was being spent on roads for motorists who represented a very small percentage of the population. Since few of Bogota's residents would ever own a car, the Mayor and his team correctly reasoned that they needed to shift the city's infrastructure so it benefited the maximum number of people. This meant an unprecedented investment in walking, bicycling and bus transit infrastructure.

Bogota did not have the funding to build modern freeways or rail-based transit. Instead, they developed a new type of urban mobility system called the TransMillennio, a bus rapid transit (BRT) system that was designed to look and operate just like rail-based transit but without the high cost. The BRT stations look like train stations and the buses are high tech. Roads were designed so the buses had their own lanes, and bikeways and pedestrian-friendly streets were connected into the system. In effect, Bogota created a new form of urban democracy through public works. As more people were able to use their city's infrastructure, Mayor Penalosa's approval ratings went steadily up. Other cities with greater resources can follow this model. Bogota's Ciclovias have become "Sunday Parkways" and similar events in cities around the world. With their new bus-bicycle-pedestrian based transportation system, Bogota created a solution that is a great example of 'third mode' ideas.

Columbia is also the home to another place that is a model for communities of any size and resource level. Gaviotas is a small, sustainable village built in a sparsely populated region above the headwaters of the Orinoco River. The story of the village was reported on National Public Radio in the 1990s and in the subsequent book, "*A Village to Reinvent the World*." When a friend of mine gave me the book, he said, "You will probably say the same thing so many others say about Gaviotas: How is it possible that I didn't know about this place before?" The founders of Gaviotas, including their leader Paolo Lugari, invented the technologies required to live in their new place. They created new solar collectors that worked on cloudy days, developed hand pumps that could retrieve fresh water from aquifers 40' below the surface, and planted sustainable forests to harvest valuable resins. They proved that with appropriate technology, it is possible to live sustainably almost anywhere on Earth.

The problem is that both Gaviotas and Bogota are not the mainstream of modern development. Relatively few people know about their innovative third mode solutions. The thinking that created these places needs to become mainstream, but our systems of thinking are slow to change. Still, there are emerging trends that are trying to move these ideas forward. As the transportation profession tries to evolve beyond the 'highways vs. transit' paradox into a more holistic approach, a new trend has emerged to create what are known as "Complete Streets." This movement started over the past decade in the U.S. and has grown to represent a vision of streets as places that are designed for people, not just their motor vehicles.

A Complete Street includes the appropriate solutions for pedestrians, bicyclists, transit customers, the disabled, freight services and other mobility needs. This is a significant departure from previous mono-modal approaches that focused primarily on motorized vehicles through a community as fast as possible. Creating this change involves re-creating a wide variety of transportation planning tools to make the design of streets into a more holistic process. Making Complete Streets happen is another example of third mode thinking being applied to create sustainable mobility solutions.

It is important to realize that the concepts of mainstream American transportation planning are embedded into our language in subtle ways. These uses of language prevent us from fully expressing basic issues about safety, equity and social needs of our public streets. It is common to hear people say that somebody was "hit by a car" when what they really mean is that somebody was "hit by a driver with a car." We say that there was an "accident" when a "crash" or "collision" is what has occurred. A "closed street" is actually a street that has been *opened* to people. The "design vehicle" that engineers frequently use for streets is usually a huge tractor trailer truck, when in urban areas the design vehicle should be a grandparent pushing a child in a stroller. Imagine the difference if your street was designed by somebody whose highest priority wasn't moving big motor vehicles through your community, but instead was focused on ensuring that parents and children can move safely.

Thinking this way requires a major change out of the fossil-fueled mindset that has evolved in our motor vehicle based society. This issue is compounded by the fact that for most of the population, the built environment is something that is experienced subconsciously. People move through their day without thinking about why their buildings and places are designed the way they are. It is only a small part of the population that spends its time trying to change the built environment, and many of these people have been trained in the past several decades during the peak of our dependence on fossil fuels. At some level, as a culture, we have lost the consciousness of understanding what makes places good, and we have trusted the engineering, architecture and landscape design professions to provide us with the built environment we inhabit. As a result, traffic engineers have ended up in a significant position to organize our lives around motorized mobility, architecture has become a fashion show that is more concerned with high art than the context of buildings, and landscape architecture has continued to perpetuate the suburban development model.

This is not to say that there aren't positive changes happening. The recent trend of New Urbanist community development has led a return to traditional town planning based on pedestrian mobility. New towns like Celebration, Florida have demonstrated that it is possible to build brand new communities in the United States that have the walkable neighborhoods which once defined the American small town. Unfortunately, the New Urbanists have generally not integrated bicycling into their new towns, and many of their projects have been built on new suburban open space instead of re-building in existing urban neighborhoods. For example, a few years ago, my firm was asked to help re-design the master plan for a New Urbanist town in Tennessee. The prominent town planner who laid out the community had included a beautiful town center for pedestrians, but did not include greenways, trails, or on-street bikeways as a part of the plan. We were asked to provide those critical layers of the town's new infrastructure. A second generation of New Urbanists is now working on a new set of planning guidelines that include bikeways and integral part of town planning and design.

To see a model where the concept of Complete Streets has been taken to the level of an art form, it is worth looking at the Dutch town of Houten. Houten is a small city of more than 50,000 residents on the outskirts of Utrecht. It is a relatively new town, and was expanded around a rural hamlet of 4,000 people as part of a regional plan developed in the 1980s. This initiative was part of the Dutch new towns movement, which included other well-planned town-centers such as Zootemeer. These new communities were based in part on the Garden Cities of post-World War II England, and were developed at the peak of modern American-styled suburbia. Houten was designed to make travel by bicycle the key mode of transportation, and today nearly half of all travel in the community is done by bike.

In addition, there has not been a traffic fatality of any kind in Houten since the community was expanded.

It is hard to believe that this is possible in a modern, high-tech community. Most of the households in Houten own cars - just like Americans - they just don't drive them everywhere they go. This was achieved by high quality urban design. Houten has a perimeter ring road for cars and trucks, but the secondary roads that go through the center of town are prioritized for bicyclists. Motorists can access every residence and business, but it isn't easy for motorists to drive across town without going back out to the ring road. Since it is easier to move within the town by bicycle, that is exactly what the residents of Houten do. Every day, trips to school, to soccer practice, to music lessons, to restaurants, to visit friends and to go shopping are all done by bike.

Every street in Houten is a Complete Street, and each one is designed to provide a function that is appropriate to the time and distance required to move sustainably. As an American, it is strange to see how normal Houten looks. The bicyclists aren't dressed in special clothing, they don't need to wear helmets all the time because their community is safe, and people of all ages are out cycling every day. The people in Houten look happy and healthy. This is true for the Dutch as a whole – in large part because they are physically active as a routine part of daily life. Houten is living proof that we can create not only Complete Streets, but Complete Communities.

In other ways, transportation is being integrated to include sustainable infrastructure solutions based on walking and bicycling. "Road Diets" have become a popular term for planners as overbuilt suburban streets are being converted with narrower lanes for motorists and well- designed space for pedestrians, transit and bicyclists. Innovative hybrids of traffic calming treatments are leading to the creation of new "Bicycle Boulevards" that combine slow-speed travel for motorists with priority for travel by bicyclists. Iconic streets like Broadway, in New York City, Pennsylvania Avenue in Washington, D.C., and Commonwealth Avenue in Boston now have dedicated bikeways, and the rate of change in creating livable streets is continuing to increase. The Institute of Transportation Engineers (ITE) recently produced a guideline on Creating Walkable Urban Thoroughfares, and the April 2011 edition of the ITE journal was simply titled "Sustainability." These are significant signs of positive change.

Since so many of the innovative streetscape treatments for bicyclists that are now being used in American cities have not been included in state and federal design guidelines, a new guide has been produced by the National Association of City Transportation Officials (NACTO). This document, the NACTO Urban Bikeway Design Guide, is a game-changer at several levels. For decades, most urban transportation design policy in the U.S. has been governed by documents produced by either State departments of transportation or the Federal government. The American Association of State Highway Transportation Officials (AASHTO) produces the "Green Book" that is considered the Bible of the transportation infrastructure profession. The Federal Highway Administration is responsible for the Manual of Uniform Traffic Control Devices (MUTCD), which regulates signage and pavement markings. Since neither document contained a wide variety of the innovative bikeway treatments being developed in cities, NACTO decided to create its own guidelines.

Numerous attempts had been made to improve the MUTCD and AASHTO guides – but both documents are only updated once in a decade, require long national review processes for new treatments, and suffer from structural inefficiencies that limit creativity. For example, AASHTO requires approvals from the 50 state Departments of Transportation (some of whom don't support improved facilities for bicyclists and pedestrians). Changing the MUTCD requires a multi-year, national committee process. The MUTCD signage and pavement marking committees don't meet together – which explains why a pavement marking for bicyclists can show a person on a bicycle, but the signs included in the MUTCD just show a bicycle without a rider. After a decade of requests, the MUTCD national committee still has not developed a guideline for bicycle traffic signals. This should be a simple thing to change, but it hasn't happened despite repeated attempts. This is due to the cumbersome process for updating the manual.

The NACTO guide recognized that these slow bureaucratic procedures were holding back innovation in cities – and that a third mode solution was necessary. Led by a core group of professionals in Portland, New York, Boston, San Francisco, Chicago, Minneapolis and other cities, NACTO commissioned my firm, Alta Planning + Design to create a new, collaborative, web-based design guide. More than twenty innovative treatments, ranging from bicycle boulevards to protected 'cycletracks' and intersection 'bike boxes' were documented, illustrated with high quality 3-D graphics, and published on the NACTO website. This process was accomplished in one year. Now cities have the design guidelines they need, without having to wait another decade for state and federal agencies to provide them. When a designer says they can't do something new because it's "not in the manual," the answer is now, "yes it is."

In some ways, the integration of transportation in the U.S. is similar to the Civil Rights movement. Isn't being able to walk safely across the street a basic human right? The protest movement of the 1960s called for black Americans to have the right to vote, to go to the same schools, and to live the same way as other citizens. I'm not saying that mobility and civil rights are issues at the same level, and the progressive transportation movement doesn't have the same level of societal power, but the goals are similar: for people to be able to freely use any mode of travel they choose. Pedestrians, bicyclists and transit customers should have the same rights as motorists – but the design of our built environment has not provided that equal opportunity. The growing Complete Streets movement in the U.S. is creating momentum to adopt the policies, legislation and programs to turn this vision into reality.

Achieving this cultural-level change requires a leap beyond the current oppositional framework of bi-modal politics. Transportation advocacy has often been based on adversarial strategies. The bicyclists are fighting against the motorists, pedestrians are fighting against the bicyclists, motorists are anti-transit. It's an endless back and forth amongst perceived opposites, when in reality, all modes of travel share common ground. Everyone wants to get from place to place safely. Everyone wants the freedom to choose a form of travel that is appropriate. In fact, most people don't fit into a single mode of travel such as 'bicyclist' or 'motorist.' Our needs change every day and throughout our lives – sometimes people ride bikes, take a bus, ride a train, walk or drive. We use different modes of travel at different times - the challenge is not how one mode can be superior, but how all modes can coexist.

One new organization that has tapped into this broader mobility perspective is the Share the Road Coalition (STR) in Ontario. The group's philosophy refers back to the history of the Better Roads Movement in the 1890s, when bicyclists first lobbied for paved roads in the U.S. The STR Coalition was founded by Eleanor McMahon, after her husband was killed on his bicycle by a person driving a truck in 2006. Eleanor was not new to high-level politics. She was Press Secretary to the Canadian Prime Minister Jean Chrétien, and had served as Director of Public Affairs at Petro-Canada, Vice President Communications and Marketing at the Canadian Chamber of Commerce and Vice President Marketing and Communications at United Way Ottawa. She knew that in order to turn her tragedy into action, she needed to find a way beyond conventional advocacy.

Eleanor had seen how ineffective the traditional 'us vs. them' politics had been in Toronto and Ottawa. Many bike advocates, frustrated from years of effort to get their communities to change, had created adversarial relationships with community leaders. While there is a place for aggressive tactics such as protests and civil disobedience, Eleanor saw a new role for advocacy based on third mode thinking. Instead of rallying bicyclists to fight against politicians for change, she found allies to establish new partnerships. The Share the Road coalition involves a wide range of groups that support safety, economic development and quality of life. The word 'bicycle' is intentionally missing from the organization's name.

McMahon's organization has had significant accomplishments in just a few years – new legislation has been passed, new projects are moving forward, and new partners are getting involved because they share the broader perspective of "Share the Road." For example, a powerful group of Canadian leaders in the financial industry has provided support for the Coalition. They are known as "Les Domestiques," after the name for the support riders in elite bicycle racing. The group was co-founded by Tim Hockey, who is the President and CEO of TD Canada Trust, a global financial institution. He is an avid bicyclist, but was informed by his company's risk management team that he would no longer be allowed to ride because bicycling was an "unsafe activity" for a key executive. Tim decided it was time to support advocacy that would change this attitude towards him and his fellow cyclists. He wanted to make the roads safe. Tim and Eleanor connected because Les Domestiques and Share the Road shared the kind of common ground that could lead to making communities safer. Now both organizations are collaborating in powerful ways that could not have happened with prior forms of adversarial-based advocacy.

Even with the rise of innovations such as Complete Streets and new third-mode advocates like the Share the Road coalition, there are still major cultural obstacles to changing the status quo. No single solution will instantly change the automobile-oriented development pattern of the United States into the great cities of Europe overnight. The same is true in reverse – the great cities of Europe and other nations need to avoid the automobile-oriented sprawl of American-style suburbia. There is a wide range of infrastructure, land use, and economic issues intertwined in these issues. Some of Europe's urban centers

(Dresden and Rotterdam for example) were destroyed in WWII and have been rebuilt in the same half-century that suburban sprawl dominated the American landscape. If post war Europe could rebuild its cities into great places, then it is possible that Detroit, Buffalo, Cleveland and other post-industrial American cities can use the potential of their current conditions to create sustainable solutions in the next generation.

Part of solving this challenge comes from changing the fact that the built environment is a subconscious experience to most people. We need a new generation of professionals in architecture, urban planning, engineering and landscape architecture, who are aware of the effect that the built environment has on how society moves, thinks and feels. We need new leaders who look at their streets and say to themselves, "We should add bike lanes here, put in a bus shelter and fix these sidewalks and crosswalks." We cannot continue to assume that the way most Americans live - using their cars for the majority of travel every day- is the way things have always been, and the way that they should be. To paraphrase twice from Winston Churchill, 'we shape our communities and they in turn shape us,' and, 'you can 'trust the Americans to find the solution to every problem, but only after they have tried every other possible alternative.' Integrating transportation with Complete Streets is a third mode way of finding these solutions.

# 7. SAFE ROUTES TO SCHOOLS

## It's Hard to be a Saint in the Suburbs

There is a growing international movement to encourage more people to be physically active in response to the world's obesity epidemic, traffic safety and environmental issues. One of the more innovative fronts in this movement is called Safe Routes to Schools, which is based on trying to get more kids to walk and bike to school more often. This is a great program that is literally changing the lives of a generation of students. Unfortunately, changing the existing system of school mobility can be incredibly frustrating for many communities. Ingrained patterns of decision making at multiple levels can create significant resistance. This is true from elementary schools through the university system in the U.S. Even a simple 'mom and apple pie' program aimed at making communities safer for children can run into institutionalized opposition. Understanding what is happening inside this issue provides another useful example of third mode thinking.

At some level, the issues that we talk about globally have to make some connection personally. If our society is going to deal with the big issues like climate change, energy independence and physical inactivity, part of the solution must take place at the local level. I believe that every day, most people in the developed nations of the world have at least some chance to make a personal change that affects broader issues. This is why I turn out the lights when I leave a room, it's why I recycle, and it's why my family tries to eat locally grown organic food as much as possible. When it comes to mobility, there is no greater microcosm of these big picture issues coming home to roost than in the way children move in their communities. When I was born, the majority of American children walked, biked, took school buses or used public transportation to get to school. Today, with the exception of large cities, most American children are driven to school in cars or buses by adults.

This change has resulted in an entire generation of children who do not have the ability to navigate independently and who don't like transit because of their experiences riding the yellow school bus. They are being raised by a generation of parents who grew up in the suburbs and now spend a large portion of their day driving their kids around. Clearly this is both a cultural issue and a result of the physical design of suburban America. The way I grew up in Paramus, New Jersey is a good example. American suburbs were originally sold as places with clean air, open spaces and the ability to buy an affordable home with a nice back yard. Kids were supposed to grow up safe, and the classic Norman Rockwell-esque image of suburbia was of a young boy delivering newspapers along a tree lined street. This image did not fully match the reality of growing up in Paramus.

We lived in a prototypical suburban neighborhood, on a local street that connected to a collector street that in turn led to two bigger roads and then on to the highway. There was no down-town. Everyone had to drive everywhere, almost all the time. I delivered newspapers by bike, but riding across town wasn't easy because you had to cross the big highway. There was one significant exception. We walked or biked to school almost every day. The solution that was in place to make our collector street, Roosevelt Boulevard, into a safe school zone when I went to elementary school is something that I can't even imagine proposing in an American suburb today.

In Paramus during the 1960s, Roosevelt Boulevard had my elementary school at one end, busy roads at both ends, and our Middle School and town swimming pool in the middle. Every morning before school started, a railroad mast arm gate was lowered in front of the Middle School, preventing motorists from driving the full length of Roosevelt Boulevard. The gate was opened again in the afternoon before the evening rush hour. During the day, people could still drive from either end of the Boulevard to the middle, and school buses had access to both schools. Because there were so few cars on the road, kids from the surrounding neighborhoods walked or biked along the Boulevard to school every day, and went home for lunch, too. We did this without our parents having to drive us, without having to use school buses for short-distance trips, and we had the freedom to safely travel through our neighborhood.

Can you even imagine going into a suburban New Jersey neighborhood today and proposing to put a railroad gate across the middle of a busy collector road? I doubt that today's residents in that neighborhood would even believe that the gate ever existed, let alone that it worked beautifully, and that all the kids living in that neighborhood in the 1960s got to walk and bike to school. It was a win-win, third mode solution for everyone – commuters could drive their cars in the morning and evening, kids got some fresh air and exercise every day, the school district saved money by not having to provide buses for kids living near the school, parents didn't have to provide taxi service for their kids, and the neighborhood got a safe, quiet street.

Unfortunately, the railroad gate solution on Roosevelt Boulevard wasn't destined to last. Before I finished Middle School, our neighbors across the street led a successful petition to have the gate removed. They didn't have young children and wanted to drive their cars all the time. As it turned out, so did most of the adults in the neighborhood. Unfortunately, those decisions did not fully consider the effect on local children, and the long term consequences of taking away their freedom of mobility. This kind of decision was being made all across the suburban American landscape of the 1960s. These decisions added up over time to create a society where it became virtually impossible for most people to walk or bike anywhere.

My father and a few other commuters in our neighborhood walked across a weedy strip mall parking lot each morning to the edge of the State highway, Route 17, to take the Shortline bus into New York City. For a while, when the suburbs of New Jersey were new, the bus made that trip into the City in half an hour. The highway was almost bucolic, with a grassy center median, and local two lane roads crossed it without traffic lights or overpasses. By the time I graduated high school, the same trip into New York could take more than an hour because of the traffic jams caused by suburban sprawl. Route 17 in Paramus became the poster child of the American suburban highway, lined with shopping malls that had replaced all of the local farmland.

While I was growing up, that Shortline bus was the only public transit available in our town. Until we were old enough to drive, we had only a few options for getting around: get a ride from somebody, walk or bike, or take the bus to the Port Authority Bus Terminal on 42nd Street in Manhattan. At that time, 42nd Street was one of the world's most decadent places: full of sex shops, drug dealers and crime. It was as far from American middle class suburbia as you could possible get, but as kids we still took the bus into the city anyway. At least we didn't have to ask for a ride. If you didn't have a car, or a friend with a car, getting a ride was always a little demeaning, and took away the feeling of independence that youth need to feel. I'll never forget having to get a ride from my father to take a girl to the movies, because there was no other way for us to get there. Without a car, I felt trapped in suburbia.

Most places in Paramus were too far away to walk to, except the nearby strip mall. I tried to be that Rockwell-esque kid riding around on my Stingray bike, and cutting lawns with my brother. I saved up enough money to buy my first "real" bike, a Sears Free Spirit 10-speed, and that became my true source of mobility. I biked with friends all over the North Jersey suburbia, on roads that today's parents would be horrified to let their kids out on. We would bike north through Bergen County to Tice's Farm for apple cider and doughnuts – a full day adventure on two-lane county roads. I biked across town to soccer practice, getting some extra physical activity on the way.

By the time I was in high school, I had a job flipping burgers at the Paramus Park Mall. I biked to work along the highway shoulder of Route 17 and across the mall entrance ramp to work. I had no headlights, no helmet, and no idea how unsafe it was to be a bike commuter in suburban America. Until I had a driver's license, my social life was limited to places where I could get to by the transportation choices available in suburbia: the school bus, getting rides from people who had cars, the bus to 42nd Street, walking and bicycling. Since I came from a family that did not have the resources to buy me a car, there was no alternative.

Times change. By the time I went to college, I had saved enough money to help pay for my education and buy a car in my junior year. My elementary school had been sold to a Japanese industrial consortium. They needed a place to educate the children of executives from the major corporate headquarters that they had built on the site of the Ford auto plant that once employed many of our neighbors. Tice's Farm is now a suburban office park, and today, children from my neighborhood are bused and driven to school. This pattern has repeated itself throughout the United States. As Chrissie Hynde of The Pretenders put it in a song about her home state, "I went back to Ohio, and the countryside was gone."

This change happened in just one generation, from the time I was born to the time I graduated high school. The quiet suburban roads that I once biked on are now crammed with motorists, many of them driving their kids everywhere - because there is so much traffic that it's no longer safe to bike. Schools have become air quality 'hot spots' because of the bus fumes and all the idling cars. Parents are afraid to let their kids travel on their own out of fear from crime, kidnappings and safety. Planners and engineers have created a transportation system where people too old or too young to drive are dependent on other people to drive them around. A new generation has grown up not knowing the freedom of travelling independently, and they are now running the school boards and local governments.

I am now a parent of three children, and we live in Saratoga Springs, a former Victorian-era resort community that is part of the fastest growing suburban county in upstate New York. We are living through a new generation of decision making that is typical of many small cities in America. Saratoga has 25,000 residents, many of whom commute by car to the State Capital in Albany. The local school district encompasses the City and the surrounding suburban towns of Wilton and Greenfield. We live in what is called the "Inner District" – the historic downtown of gridded tree lined streets, traditional homes with front porches, and within walking distance of the commercial center of town on Broadway. We have a beautiful central park a few blocks away, and an elementary school six blocks away. Sounds ideal, right? Wouldn't you assume that all of our kids walk or bike to school like we once did?

All of the kids in our neighborhood are provided with buses to go to school. Few of the kids, and especially the ones that are older than third grade, want to ride the bus. It takes too long, there is bad behavior by other kids on the bus, and they don't like the bus schedule. Some families walk, but many parents drive their kids six blocks to school. The school is a former urban high school from the 1920's, on a small neighborhood site. The former courtyard at the center of the school is now used as a parking lot for teachers. The streets around the school are jammed with parents picking up their kids in cars and SUVs before and after school. The curbs alongside the school entrance were removed so motorists can drive right up next to the sidewalk and drop of children. Many of these motorists are our neighbors. Even so, this school has the highest percentage of walkers and bike riders in the district. It is far worse at the other elementary schools that are not in the Inner District.

The decisions that led to these conditions are the result of a suburban generation that can't imagine walking and bicycling to school as a real solution for transportation. The current school board does not have a single representative from the City's Inner District. The decisions that they are making are based on a suburban mono-modal way of thinking that assumes that the only way to go anywhere is in a motor vehicle. As a result, school busing is now a significant item in the annual budget. Every year the school board approves another major bond issue for new school buses – at a cost of nearly $1 million dollars per year. Our community recently voted to approve bonding for a new school bus garage, but failed to approve funding for a swimming pool. Motorized travel to school has become an assumption.

The Middle School in Saratoga is an even more incredible story. Maple Avenue Middle School serves the entire school district, and was built (like so many suburban American schools) on cheap land along a suburban State road at the edge of town. When the school was built, an old dirt road from the end of

North Broadway served as a trail, and bike racks were installed at the back of the school near the trail. At the front of the school, the school board wanted the State to install a traffic light at the main entrance. The State rejected the request, in part because the only traffic issue on the road was going to be all the cars and buses from the school. Since the signal couldn't be provided, the school board thought that there was no safe way for kids to cross the busy road. The school decided the best option was to provide bus service for every student.

In order to get State funding for busing students who technically lived close enough to walk or bike to school, the district had to declare the area around the school a "School Safety Zone." In New York State law, this Orwellian term is defined as an area where it is unsafe to walk or bike, so children can be bused for shorter distances than would usually be allowed. There is no provision in the law for using that same funding to improve conditions in the Safety Zone so that it would become a place where children could safely walk and bike to school. Maple Avenue Middle School was declared a Safety Zone in the 1990s. In order to approve the Safety Zone designation, the school administration banned students from bicycling or walking to school, and required that all students be bused to school. While this may have made some sense in regard to the need for a signal in front of the school, it ignored the fact that a beautiful trail led directly to the back of the school.

For many years, students followed the rules and everybody took the bus to school. A handful of kids would occasionally ride their bikes or walk, and they kept a low profile. The trail gradually fell into disrepair, and the public was unsure if it was even open for use. Mountain bikers who had accessed the trail from the north end of Broadway created some controversy when they began cutting new trails on the adjacent campus of Skidmore College. The College environmental program succeeded in banning mountain bikes from the trails on campus as part of an effort to protect the area, which is called the North Woods. Many people in the community eventually assumed that this part of the college campus included the trail to the school, but that was not true. The trail is technically a City-owned public right of way. Meanwhile, the school district continued providing funding for buses, and many parents continued driving their kids to school.

Then, one day a few years ago, a Middle School student named Adam biked to school with his mother, Janette. It happened to be Bike to Work Day in Saratoga, a local attempt to try to encourage more people to ride their bikes for transportation. After dropping off her son at school, Janette got a call from the school Principal. He told her that her son had violated the school board policy by biking to school. He told her that she should go home, get a car and drive him home. Adam's bike, which was locked outside the school, had been impounded. Janette is not shy, and she is a force to be reckoned with. She alerted local advocates and the media, and publicly raised the issue of how little sense it made for a school to ban kids from bicycling to school. If logic was the basis for making decisions, this story should have been enough for the School District to change its policy immediately, right?

Unfortunately, the School District dug in its heels and stood by its policy, and publicly re-stated their policy that students were prohibited from biking or walking to school. Janette and her family soon became the focal point of a protracted community battle that could only happen in today's suburban America. The School Board reluctantly agreed to form a task force to investigate the issue. Since the Board was comprised primarily of suburban members, and the task force included all of the suburban elementary schools where children are primarily driven or bused to school, it was difficult to make the case that children should be walking and biking to school. The arguments for improved health, physical activity, connections to nature, and cost savings on buses fell on deaf ears. The board insisted that, "it simply wasn't safe" and that the only solution was to bus or drive every child to school.

I volunteered to help the task force draft a new policy, and tried to apply some third mode thinking. We recognized that each of the district's schools had unique conditions that needed to be addressed. The Middle School had both the trail on one side (which by this time few people even knew existed) and the State road on the other. Each elementary school had different issues – some of the schools had been built in suburban locations on two lane roads, but others were in walkable downtown neighborhoods. The new policy was drafted to reflect these conditions and included a simple three-part process: schools would be designated as either 'green' – safe to walk or bike to school under current conditions, 'yellow' – needs relatively minor improvements that could be made within a few years, or 'red' – not safe and requires major improvements. Each school would produce its own action plan, with the overall goal of making all of the schools 'green' within five years.

While this could have been a good resolution to the problem, that again proved not to be the case. The School Board balked at the idea that the task force had even presented a new policy. They claimed that only the School Board members could develop policies, and the task force was only supposed to provide information to the board. Even though the task force offered to find funding for the improvements through the national Safe Routes to Schools program, even though the concept was flexible, it still represented a change from the way things were being done. Nearly a year went by, during which another class of students went through Middle School in Saratoga without the opportunity to walk or bike to school.

The story continued to get mentioned in the media, and finally the School Board agreed to have the issue on the agenda for one of its meetings. As the meeting approached, the new policy received editorial support from local papers, and then got national attention when Newt Gingrich, the former Speaker of the House of Representatives (who had seen the story online and was working on health care reform issues) wrote to the Albany Times Union advocating for Saratoga to become a model for helping to make children more physically active by encouraging them to walk or bike to school. Adam's story had gone viral, and it seemed like the national media exposure would finally break through the morass of local mono-modal thinking.

Again, this should have been enough to provide a happy ending to the story, but the power of suburban thinking is strong. At the School Board meeting where the proposed policy change was finally presented, the Board pulled a complete end run around the local Safe Routes to Schools advocates. Instead of putting the policy on the agenda for public discussion, it was approved as a 'consent agenda' item without open debate. This happened so quickly that people in the audience thought that the new policy submitted by the task force had been approved by the full school board. Again, this was false hope. I finally managed to ask a question from the floor about what the text of the new policy actually said. I was told that this item was not up for discussion, but that copies had been provided to the media in attendance. This was a shock, because the document had not been provided to any of the members of the task force. It was clear that something was up.

When a copy of the new policy document was located, it was a completely different version than what the task force had proposed. The School Board had modified their existing ban to grudgingly allow students to walk or bike to school, but only if they were accompanied by a parent, had filed a written permission form with the school, walked their bikes while on school property, and individual school principals had the authority to continue banning walking and bicycling at their discretion. There was no mention of improving conditions at the schools, and no program to encourage children to participate. The Board was able to publicly claim that they had voted to change the policy, without anybody knowing the changes that they had made. To try to be fair to the Board members who took this action, in their opinion they were acting in the interest of safety for the students. They simply did not believe that walking or bicycling to school was a good idea.

Unfortunately, the suburban School Board did not have the perspective of people who lived in a place where walking and bicycling could be safe, normal, fun everyday activities. This same is true for many suburban communities in the U.S. They do not think that the benefits of supporting new solutions will outweigh the potential liabilities they perceive. The Saratoga task force is still meeting occasionally, and has made some basic improvements such as providing bike racks at some schools, making the required forms available to parents, and trying to steer the slow moving local policy process. But the Saratoga school district and its peers across the country have a long way to go before the majority of students, faculty and staff walk and bike to school. Another class of students will go through the school system in Saratoga and communities like it throughout the U.S. this year. It may take an entire generation before the old thinking can finally be replaced by progressive solutions. School bus companies will oppose Safe Routes programs because of perceived job and budget losses. Lawyers will advise school boards that it is a liability for kids to walk or bike to school. Parents will continue to live in either real or perceived fear that their children can't walk or bike to school safely. Kids will continue to think it isn't cool to bike to school. Meanwhile, another generation of Americans will continue to be obese, dependent on fossil fuels, and will fail to be part of the solutions to critical global issues including climate change, health care and energy dependence.

There will be communities (and kids) who are winners and losers in this process. There are many places around the world that are successfully implementing Safe Routes to Schools programs. The Safe Routes movement started in Odense, Denmark and moved to the U.K., where it became a national success. In the U.S., Marin County, California; Arlington, Virginia; and other communities created pilot projects that have led to a national program. Safe Routes to Schools received more than $700 million in the last federal transportation bill, and successful projects have happened throughout the U.S. But these projects are only the tip of the iceberg, and for most communities in America, there is still a long way to go.

It is completely possible that I am wrong and the communities that resist these changes are right, but there is a growing body of research that backs up what common sense should tell us: kids who walk and bike to school are more physically active, perform better in school and learn skills that kids who are driven in cars or buses do not. Safety data show us that it is dangerous to be a passenger in a motor vehicle, and behavior on school buses is a constant issue. For parents who are afraid that their kids will be abducted, many schools have created safety patrols, walking school buses and bike trains where volunteers serve as chaperones. Any of the issues that maintain monomodal thinking can be resolved if there is a willingness to find the solution.

It is interesting to note that Portland, Oregon went through a similar phase with their schools. In the 1990s, Portland also banned kids from biking to school. The difference in Portland was that progressive leaders were making their city a center of innovation on a wide variety of issues including land use, technology and transportation. Activists didn't just get the school board to vote on a new policy, they got it done by voting out the board members who were in the opposition. Today, Portland is working on initiatives to make it possible for the majority of students, faculty and staff to bike and walk to school. It is common to see teenagers moving freely throughout the city on their bikes, riding transit, and getting around without depending on adults all of the time. This generation of citizens will have a different future. They are a decade ahead of the communities that have not seen this future yet. They will realize the health, environmental, economic, and quality of life benefits of these changes sooner than other places. In a world where innovation and change are keys to the future, these decisions may be the proverbial fork in the road.

These are not just issues for the elementary, middle and high school levels. Since 1996, I have been teaching a course called "Bicycling, Walking and Trails: Innovations in Transportation" at the State University of New York at Albany (UAlbany). This course was the first graduate-level University bicycle and pedestrian planning course of its kind in the U.S. The experience of teaching this course offers important insights into the future of sustainable mobility. If we are going to create a new generation of leaders who think in the third mode, that change has to happen at all levels of education.

I started teaching at UAlbany while I was working as New York State's Bicycle and Pedestrian Program Manager. NYSDOT was looking to hire people with experience in bicycle/pedestrian transportation for regional offices and Metropolitan Planning Organizations (MPO's). I contacted Professor Ray Bromley at UAlbany's School of Geography and Planning and asked him if he had any students trained in this subject. He said no, and he didn't know of any school in the U.S. teaching such a course. He then said, 'but if you want to start doing this, write up a syllabus and you can teach the course here at UAlbany.'

That initial meeting at UAlbany has led to fifteen years of rewarding teaching and learning. The students who have graduated from our program have gone on to a wide variety of key positions, including two State DOT bicycle and pedestrian coordinators, a Federal Highway Administration (FHWA) planning director, staff at the NYC Department of Transportation, a national fellowship winner who worked for Congressman Earl Blumenauer of Oregon, a coordinator for the Institute of Transportation Engineers' sustainable mobility program, several MPO staff, leaders of advocacy organizations, consultants for firms throughout the U.S., a statewide campus planner for the California University system and many others. As other similar programs evolve in the U.S. and internationally, this will be an important benchmark for them: how have your students changed the world?

It is important to state that there have been a number of efforts to expand this initiative to other Universities in the U.S. and internationally. Before I started teaching, my first step was to reach out via email to contacts across the U.S. to see who else was offering a similar course. When I got no reply, I sent the email again because at that time the internet was so new that I thought my message hadn't been sent properly. I finally got a message from a professor at the University of Washington. He said that he'd been working on a course that centered around bicycling from an engineering perspective, but he'd also been unable to find anyone teaching a full course on walking and bicycling for transportation at the university level. It was both exciting and sobering that our course at UAlbany would be the first in the nation.

After a couple of years of teaching at UAlbany, other efforts began to develop. I was among a core group of leaders that co-founded the Association of Bicycle and Pedestrian Professionals (APBP) and we made the development of a national bicycle and pedestrian course at the University level one of our new organization's national priorities. The FHWA had begun work on a national course curriculum with a team of consultants. Other innovators, including Alex Sorton at Northwestern offered technical seminars on walking and bicycling, and Linda Crider at the University of Florida began a similar semester long bike and pedestrian course. Through APBP, we shared the original UAlbany course materials with other schools, and I was asked to give the first lecture at the University of Florida when they started their program.

The FHWA curriculum project took a number of years to develop, and in the early 2000's other schools began offering courses (including UC Berkeley and Portland State). During that time we kept on teaching the course at UAlbany. Guest lecturers included national leaders such as Dan Burden of Florida, Michael Ronkin from Oregon, Tim Young from Jackson Hole, Ivan Vamos of the New York Bike Coalition and others.

As my career changed gears (I had left NYSDOT in 1998 to serve as director of the US Millennium Trails Program, and later became a partner with Alta Planning + Design) we continued to keep the course in the UAlbany catalogue. In 2001, I worked with Professor Catherine Lawson to help UAlbany get a major grant from the NYS Department of Health to fund the Initiative for Healthy Infrastructure (iHi). The iHi program developed action plans for communities to connect public health with public works, and published guidelines that have helped establish Complete Streets and

Safe Routes to Schools policies at the local, regional and state levels. One of the strengths of our work at UAlbany – and a constant factor in student evaluations – has been the combination of professional experience with academic teaching. This has been both a challenge and an opportunity as a working professional who teaches part-time. It has been difficult to maintain the time in my busy schedule to still be able to teach. I have not always been able to serve on academic committees, write journal articles, and spend extra time on campus. I did chair a session at the VeloMondiale 2000 conference in Amsterdam on international education, served on several Transportation Research Board (TRB) committees, offered my time as an advisor to the team developing the FWWA course, and we have always made our UAlbany program available on-line. However, my academic life is not a full time job, and that limits how much can be accomplished. At the same time, teaching is a very rewarding experience that has been worth every minute. Our course has consistently been fully subscribed and has always received evaluations that place it among our students' favorite courses.

As the UAlbany program has evolved, we have also been able to integrate the bicycle and pedestrian curriculum into the graduate planning studio program. The studio allows students to work with professionals and local communities on real projects. Recent studios have included a plan for the "Purple Path" around the UAlbany campus, a Main Street Plan for the village of Sugar Loaf, New York, a traffic calming study for Old Bennington, Vermont and a trail linking communities in the Hudson River Valley. These practical projects have informed the structure of our academic course, and the importance of 'real world' projects has been a real strength of the planning program. The UAlbany syllabus has evolved with student input so that the course now is taught with a two part framework. The first half of the semester is presented as a lecture format course (using original materials supplemented by the FHWA national curriculum). The second half of the course is then led by the students working on and presenting case studies and interactive projects.

In recent years, other schools have increased the offerings of similar courses in the U.S. An updated version of the national course based on the FHWA curriculum has been developed by the University of North Carolina. Portland State (with a team that includes my business partner Mia Birk) has established the Institute for Bicycle and Pedestrian Infrastructure – IBPI. In addition to my consulting work and teaching at UAlbany, I have had the honor of guest lecturing at a number of other schools, including Syracuse, Cornell, University of Virginia, University of Florida, Vienna Institute of Technology (BOKU), Skidmore College, and Rensselaer Polytechnic Institute. The next generation of university programs is a key development in creating sustainable, livable, healthy communities for the future. Based on fifteen years of actively teaching this subject, I offer the following ideas as potential next steps:

**Link Funding to Teaching Sustainable Mobility:** Every school that receives federal transportation research funding can integrate walking and bicycling into their academic program. This can be accomplished at minimal cost within those programs by including a course in each school's annual work program, using the materials developed by FHWA and others.

**Expand to a Full Curriculum:** Beyond just a three-credit course on walking and bicycling, a comprehensive sustainable mobility curriculum can be developed with individual sections on walking, bicycling, transit, Complete Streets, Safe Routes to Schools and other related programs. Portland State's IBPI is working on this concept and multiple schools can offer similar programs.

**Integrate Real Projects:** Students have constantly said that the combination of real-world experience and academics is the key to the UAlbany course. In order for this to be possible, working professionals must take part in teaching to support the next generation.

**Connect with Innovative Programs:** We can work with universities to link on-campus sustainability programs with teaching courses and the new Bicycle Friendly Campus initiative from the League of American Bicyclists. These are great new opportunities to combine teaching with creating livable communities.

**Active Teaching:** every class is an opportunity to engage students, faculty and communities in activities that are participatory experiences. Charrettes, walking audits, bike facilities tours, and related activities are important, especially in regards to growing support for active transportation and recreation.

**Globalize/Technologize:** the use of web-based teaching tools and communications technologies can increase the opportunity to network academics, professionals and students in a more global learning experience. We know that there are people around the world working on sustainable mobility, the challenge is to connect their efforts.

To underscore how important it is to create the next generation of "third mode" leaders on college campuses, I keep thinking about an episode that took place at Skidmore College in Saratoga Springs a decade ago. During the semester after 9/11 happened, Skidmore students voiced concern for a major issue on campus: parking their cars. The headlines of the student newspaper called for a temporary construction area in front of the Campus Center to be used as the "Freedom Lot" so more parking spaces would be available. Students were parking their cars for free on this lot, and they thought that this should be made permanent. I was stunned that this was even an issue, especially in a community that was only 175 miles from Ground Zero.

I don't expect the next generation of college students will all be visionaries, but arguing for the freedom to have more car parking spaces on campus seemed to be completely out of perspective in light of current events and global trends. At some level, I'm hoping that more college students will be involved in creating renewable energy, low-carbon lifestyles and sustainability on campus. In 2010, Skidmore asked me to serve as guest faculty to teach a course on Sustainable Mobility. The class developed its own plan for green infrastructure, including solutions that could make the campus a model for walking and bicycling for transportation, recreation and quality of life.

This was a big step forward for the same campus that had rallied for the Freedom Parking Lot in 2001. During the semester, I had a quote from a student on a mid-term essay that sums up this topic perfectly, and it went something like this: 'before this class, I hardly noticed the built environment around me. Now I can see how everything connects, and why walking and bicycling are so important.' Hearing that not only made my day, it made it worth teaching for the last 15 years – and into the future. If there is ever going to be a place where third mode thinking helps change our society, it is our classrooms. Whether the issue is getting our children to walk and bike to school, or getting out planners, designers and future leaders to think beyond our mono-modal culture, there are plenty of opportunities for education to be part of the third mode solution to global issues.

# 8. THE END OF NATURE

## Jackson Hole Community Pathways

In the mid-1990s, I first met Bill McKibben, the author of the landmark book, "The End of Nature." We met through mutual friends, and since Bill lived nearby in the Adirondacks, we went hiking and skiing together a few times. In 1995, I asked him to help me with the first New York State Bicycle and Pedestrian conference. Even though we had no budget for the event, Bill agreed to join our keynote dinner panel along with authors James Howard Kunstler, Marcia Lowe, and Tony Hiss. It was an extraordinary event. Bill talked about how the idea of the human and natural environments as separate concepts had merged into a deeply interconnected system capable of changing our earth's climate. He asked the audience if human beings, the species that is defined by its ability to walk upright, were going to someday evolve into a new creature whose right foot is bent at an angle to fit the accelerator of our automobiles. I knew then that these ideas were connected to my work making communities more walkable and bikeable.

Walking and bicycling are individual actions that can be part of a positive response to climate change. The challenge to realizing this potential is that American society has drifted so far away from living in communities where this change is possible. We live in a world where children and adults are suffering from "nature deficit disorder," a term developed by author Richard Louv in his book "Last Child in the Woods." Driving a car has become an assumption - something that we do so often, as such a part of our daily routine, that we've forgotten that there is a third mode alternative. We drive to work, to school, for shopping and socializing. We even drive for recreation, and it's common for Americans to spend their weekends using gasoline powered off-road vehicles, four wheel drive trucks, powerboats, jet skis and a wide variety of motorized outdoor activities. The common term 'Sport Utility Vehicle" has become a classic oxymoron. Even a 'Recreational Vehicle' has come to be defined as huge motor home that can be driven around the landscape as a form of motorized outdoor adventure.

The environmental movement has struggled with this issue. I had an opportunity to illustrate this point when I was asked to speak at the 75th Anniversary of the Adirondack Mountain Club (ADK). The ADK is an organization that I support, and I am currently a member. Meanwhile, it is no secret that the majority of club members drive their cars to get to the trails they enjoy. ADK members are often a part of the traffic jams on the highways leading to the Adirondack Park on weekends. One of the signature achievements of hikers in the ADK is to hike all 46 of the High Peaks in the Adirondacks. The people who accomplish this goal are called "46ers" and are considered among the elite hikers in the club. I would argue that few of them could have become 46ers without their cars.

In my speech at the 75th anniversary event, I offered a new vision for the Adirondacks. I asked the ADK members to imagine a future where the Adirondack Park is managed like the Lake District National Park in England, where the trailheads start in villages, and you hike from town to town. An ADK 46er in the future would hike the High Peaks by starting on Main Street in Lake Placid, or in hamlets like Keene Valley. Remote trailheads that make it possible to drive into the wilderness and hike from parking lots in the forest would be removed. Hikers would have to reach the high peaks from the centers of towns. This would solve the problem of "over hiking" on crowded trails and limit the environmental damage of too many people trampling the fragile summit ecosystems.

When I visited the village of Ambleside in England's Lake District in 1992, they had allowed owners of row houses on their High Street to convert rooms into bed-and-breakfast rentals. The row houses had been linked to a common reservation system, and a National Park trailhead was located at the end of the street. This arrangement functioned better than the typical roadside motels outside of many American parks, and eliminated the need to drive a car to the trailhead. It was possible to walk down the street in Ambleside, hike through the Lake District to the town of Troutbeck, have dinner at the famous Mortal Man Pub, and then hike back to my B&B in the evening. This is a great model of integrated planning and third-mode thinking. It is a potential model for the future of the Adirondack Park.

I told the audience at the ADK event that there wasn't really a problem with "over hiking" in the Adirondacks, but there was a problem with "over driving" – and that we were part of the problem. Needless to say, this was not a popular idea with that audience, and I was practically booed off the podium for mentioning it. I was mainly trying to make a point that there could be significant value in connecting the Adirondack trails system directly into the centers of towns, instead of making it so easy to drive a car into the woods to start every hike. If we are going to be part of the sustainable future, leadership of that change has to come from within the members and organizations of the environmental movement.

I know that the ADK makes a lot of its revenue operating the Adirondack Loj on Heart Lake in the High Peaks, miles from any town. It is the base camp for many 46ers. In fact, I am writing this chapter of my book on a laptop in a lean-to at Adirondack Loj after hiking the 5,000 foot Mount Algonquin with my 11 year old son. We, like so many others, could not have done that hike without driving on the interstate highway and up the State maintained roads into the mountains to this remote trailhead. But, not every trip into "nature" has to begin by driving a car – and there are successful communities creating positive connections between people and the environment as part of daily life.

When Tim Young called me from Jackson Hole, Wyoming in the spring of 2001, his community was in crisis. Two people had been killed while bicycling on local roads. One was a young girl who was on a bicycle tour with her family in Grand Teton National Park. The other was an off-duty park ranger who was riding his bike on a well-known road between the Park and the center of town. Both had been run off the road and killed by motorists in broad daylight. Neither motorist was charged with a serious crime. The Jackson Hole community was shocked, saddened and prepared to do whatever it took to keep the same thing from happening again. The events that followed have created an innovative model for using the third mode to connect people and nature.

I had met Tim and the leaders of his local group Friends of Pathways through my work with the Millennium Trails project. The Jackson Hole community had been successful in getting funding from the USDOT for construction of an epic new path over the mountains of Teton Pass to connect from Wyoming into Idaho. This was not a community with small ideas. When Tim called, he suggested that I come out to Jackson and help facilitate a community-wide, open public meeting to deal with the reaction to the two fatalities. I agreed, but asked that we have a few key elements in place for this very high-risk event. The first was that we get all of the key decision makers to participate, and the second was that they be given an opportunity to respond to community concerns as part of the process.

Tim agreed, and we called the event "Take Action, Jackson!" The program was set up to fill the local Snow King hockey arena with people from throughout the community, with a panel of the leaders of the State DOT, Grand Teton National Park, US Forest Service, Teton County and the Town of Jackson on the podium. The panelists had been asked to simply sit on the stage and listen as people came to the microphone and spoke. I was asked to serve as facilitator, along with Kent Spence, a well-known leader in the community. There was widespread publicity, and when the evening of the event arrived, more than 400 people packed the arena. It was clear from the start that we were on the edge of either a successful resolution to the community's anger, or the place was going to explode into an angry mob.

The first several speakers were friends, family members and co-workers of the two victims. It was almost impossible to listen to the memorials about Gabriella Axelrad and Tim Poole, two people whose lives had ended so suddenly. The combination of emotions and the scale of the event created an enormous tension, and it was a challenge to keep the crowd under control. People called upon the panelists to build safer roads, to create a network of pathways connecting the community, to improve bike access to the National Parks and public lands around Jackson Hole, and to enforce the laws so motorists would safely share the road with bicyclists.

After more than an hour of public comment, Gretchen Long Glickman, (a local resident and board member of the National Parks Conservation Association), stepped to the microphone. I had met Gretchen previously, and we had talked before the session started. She had a personal connection to the tragic events, but had said she was going to talk about how important it was to connect bicycling, trails and America's National Parks. The minute she began to speak, she looked at me, took a deep breath, and I knew that she was about to change the entire event. In a slow, steady voice, Gretchen said that although she was supposed to be speaking in an official capacity, the time had come for her to publicly talk about something she had never talked about before. Ten years before, Gretchen's daughter had been killed while riding her bicycle.

The air went out of the room. This was a big part of why Gretchen had become such a powerful advocate for safe pathways for bicyclists – but she had never told her daughter's story in public. She told the Take Action, Jackson! audience how her silence all these years was something she regretted – especially now that two other families were going through the same pain. There wasn't a dry eye in the house, and I struggled to keep my composure as Gretchen made it clear that this must never happen again, in Jackson Hole or anywhere else. I didn't think we could get through another minute of that tension, when we were saved by an unlikely hero. Sleeter Dover, the Secretary of the Wyoming Department of Transportation, stood up from his seat on the podium, took the microphone and said, "OK. I've heard enough. What can I do to help?"

It was hard to believe what was happening. Sleeter Dover is a black former civil rights attorney from the South who had become the leader of the State DOT in Wyoming. It was like a scene out of the movie Blazing Saddles. Sleeter took out a yellow legal pad, and said to the entire audience, "I want the next group of people to come up to the microphone and tell me something specific that my agency can do to solve the problem." He said, "You tell me what to do, and I promise you to do everything possible to get it done." He looked at his fellow panelists, and they all nodded their agreement to do the same. If we had written a script, we could not have created that moment.

The next speaker turned out to be the owner of the inn where I was staying. He said that one of the major pathway projects along his road was being held up by two things – his right-of-way was needed for the path, and the State was holding up the funding until the property rights issue was resolved. He committed to donating the land on the spot, if the DOT Secretary would agree to free up the funding. Sleeter Dover wrote the item down on his legal pad and said, "Done. – What else can I do?" The energy in the room changed completely, and it was electrifying as speaker after speaker came forward and asked for improvements that might have previously seemed impossible, and the decision makers on the panel listened while the State DOT Secretary took careful notes.

The Take Action, Jackson! public forum was the catalyst that the community needed to transform tragedy into hope. The next morning, we had set up a follow-up session with the panelists and the local media. The panel was given the opportunity to write its own media release, and the local paper had agreed to publish it. I was supposed to facilitate that session, too, but Sleeter and the other agency leaders said they'd rather do it themselves. The group sat down in a room at Town Hall, and wrote up a 'top ten' list of key priority actions, and the newspaper ran the story. Within a week, major projects were moving forward. We were still a long way from making all of Teton County bicycle friendly, but the community and all of the key agencies had taken a major step forward.

After the public forum, the leaders in Jackson decided to develop a long-term Pathways Master Plan. They had already built some great projects, and clearly had a new window of opportunity to expand the growing Pathways program. My company bid on the project, and I flew out to Jackson for the interview, which happened to take place in the middle of ski season. After my presentation at the town engineering office, I walked down the street, grabbed my skis and took the chairlift to the top of Snow King Mountain. From the top, I could see the grid of downtown Jackson meet the southern edge of the National Elk

Refuge. Herds of elk were out in the meadows, and the scene was more like a painting of the West than a real view. While I was standing there on top of the mountain, my phone rang – it was the interview committee telling me that we had won the Master Plan project.

Throughout the development of the Jackson Hole Pathways Master Plan, I never forgot that image of the Town and its surrounding landscape from the top of the mountain. The Master Plan involved field work on skis, by bike, on foot and by bus to explore how to create a vision for turning a western American resort town into a great place for walking, bicycling and trails. We developed policies for providing paved shoulders on rural roads, field tested alternative widths for bike lanes on local streets, looked at connections to adjacent public lands and conducted public meetings. At one point we illustrated a vision map that showed the full system 25 years from now, with paths connecting to Grand Teton National Park, along the Flat Creek through downtown, and along the northern edge of downtown to create a loop pathway around the perimeter of Jackson. This turned out to be a very controversial idea, but for reasons I would not have expected.

The northern section of downtown Jackson has a hospital, a school, a U.S. Forest Service Visitors' center, and a residential neighborhood along the southern border of the National Elk Refuge. There is a chain link fence between the refuge and the community. It is the dividing line between people and nature. When we proposed shifting the fence line slightly north to create space for a trail between the Town and the refuge, the "environmental" community turned out in force and led the opposition to the concept. They claimed that the "natural" environment of the refuge was absolute and must be preserved to protect the animals. They did not care that the trail might create a more environmentally-friendly way for people to experience the boundary of the preserve, or that the trail would connect the visitors' center, the hospital and the school (which had already developed a small nature trail against the fence line).

We ran into similar opposition to trails connecting the town to Grand Teton National Park. Environmental scientists cited reports claiming that the trails for people would cause a loss of habitat for moose, elk, deer and other species. We asked how many large mammals were killed by motorists in the Park each year. The answer was more than 600 animals a year. It seemed hard to imagine a trail causing the loss of habitat and death of 600 moose, elk and deer. I pointed out that it was unlikely that anyone walking or riding a bicycle would ever kill a large mammal in a collision. Even the potential habitat loss seemed like a questionable argument. The roads had been in the Park for more than 75 years and nobody was calling for getting rid of the motorists because they were killing so many animals. If we treated the trails the same way as the road system, we would just build the trails and evaluate them after 75 years of experience to see if both the people and animals could coexist.

At a public meeting to discuss the trail plan, leaders of the environmental movement vocally opposed the proposed trail along the refuge. The Wildlife Refuge director loudly stated: "this Refuge is federal land – it would take an act of Congress to change that boundary." I proposed a 'third mode' solution: why not create a new 200 foot buffer zone along the refuge boundary, make sure the trail is more than 100 feet from nearby homes, allow homeowners, the school and the hospital to utilize the buffer zone to create a greater separation between them and the refuge, and then acquire three times as much open land to add to the refuge in areas farther away from Town. This would be a win-win solution for all, and with the value of land in Jackson, the private property owners probably could have been convinced to lobby for that act of Congress. The environmentalists still opposed the idea.

I was frustrated by these debates, because I have always considered myself an environmentalist. It just doesn't make sense that creating a stronger connection between people and nature was not embraced by the environmental community. Later that week, I went for a long bike ride with Tim Young into Grand Teton National Park. It was early April and the Park road was officially closed to motorists, but it had already been plowed, and locals knew that you could go around the gate to get into the Park. It was an extraordinary ride on miles of road with no cars, no motor homes, no pickup truck drivers – just lots and lots of people walking, cross-country skiing and bicycling in the Grand Teton springtime. We saw plenty of animals, including moose, elk, and a pair of coyotes who followed us at a distance for a while.

We stopped at Jackson Lake, which is a man-made reservoir formed by a dam on the Snake River. I called Bill McKibben, the author of The End of Nature, from the top of the dam, and left him a message saying that more people needed to get his book. McKibben's thesis that people and nature are so interconnected makes it clear that we can no longer hold onto the antiquated concept that we are separate. "Nature" is not some separate place that people have to be kept away from. The irony of my message to Bill was that we were standing on top of a man-made dam that had created the habitat for a National Park – and "environmentalists" were now trying to save that habitat by keeping people from building trails that would connect people and nature in a positive way. This perspective is even harder to understand when you realize that Grand Teton National Park not only has busy roads running through it, but it also features a major hotel complex and a full scale commercial airport.

We spent months carefully working through the challenges of connecting the human and natural environments in Jackson Hole. The Pathways Master Plan went through a lengthy public debate before it was adopted by the Town and County councils in 2007. Over the course of the past five years, the Jackson Hole Community Pathways system has grown to create a network of human-powered mobility that is transforming the region. They are close to implementing their 25 year vision in less than a decade, and major projects that would have been impossible just a few years ago are now under way.

The new pathway from the north end of town to Grand Teton National Park is now open to the public. A new 800' bicycle and pedestrian bridge over the Snake River is being designed. Hundreds of miles of hiking and mountain bike trails have been connected in the Grand Teton National Forest. The pathway over Teton Pass has been completed, and an even bigger vision is being planned for a trail network connecting all the way through Yellowstone and Grand Teton National Parks.

New bike lanes are being developed along the main highways through town, and a Safe Routes to Schools program is promoting physical activity for children. Jackson Hole has been designated as a Gold level Bicycle Friendly Community by the League of American Bicyclists. More people are spending time connected to nature and their neighborhoods – and they are becoming part of the solution to global issues every day.

There is still an ongoing debate in Jackson Hole between environmentalists and pathways advocates, but they are moving away from a back-and-forth argument and towards a more holistic third-mode perspective. By having a clear plan and vision for the future, the community is finding a way to get the wide range of competing interests (developers, public agencies, property owners, businesses, and advocates) to support the Pathways system. If I could point to a single factor that has made this success possible, I would say it has been their ability to successfully organize the "key triangle" of public, private and non-profit partners. The non-profit Friends of Pathways, the Town and County Pathways Program, and the local business community are all working together in Jackson Hole.

The strength of this partnership will continue to move Jackson Hole forward. More children will be able to walk, bike and ski to school. New businesses will capitalize on the green economy. People will choose to live, work and play in the region because of the new Pathways system. Over time, the development pattern of the community will shift as more people realize the value of an active lifestyle that does not depend entirely on fossil fuels. Visitors will be able to stay in downtown hotels and bike, hike or take the bus to one of the world's great National

Parks. The reduced amounts of fossil fuels and increased amounts of physical activity will become part of the solution for health care, climate change and a greener economy. This change will be accomplished not by some massive, billion dollar infrastructure project. It will be the result of community leaders finding a cost effective, third mode solution for sustainable mobility.

# 9. BICYCLING AND WALKING IN DUBAI

## Greening the Desert

Of all the projects I've been involved in, the Dubai Bike and Pedestrian Master Plans are among the best at starting an interesting conversation. In fact, when my business partner Michael Jones first suggested that we respond to a request for proposals from the Dubai Roads and Transport Authority (RTA), we really weren't sure what to make of it. Yes, the request was for a bicycle master plan. Yes, that's our business. But, Dubai? The desert oasis city with the skyscrapers, indoor skiing and artificial islands shaped like palm trees? To our knowledge this was going to be the first bicycle plan in the Middle East. So of course, we followed Michael's intuition and went after the project.

It might seem hard to imagine why one of the world's wealthiest places, located in the middle of a region that supplies much of the world's petroleum, would want to do a bike plan. At the same time, if you understand Dubai's vision of a modern, global city that is the contemporary equivalent of ancient Rome, 19th century London or 20th century New York, it begins to make sense. The Dubai airport is becoming the world's largest. They have built the world's tallest building. The world's richest horse

195

race is held in Dubai. This is a place that wants to be a world leader. They see sustainable mobility as part of their vision.

We submitted our proposal and won the project. Brett Hondorp, the youngest of our company's partners, and at the time the only one of us without children, agreed to be our project manager and lead the project on the ground in Dubai. I can't say enough about how well Brett handled this incredibly challenging project. He managed the travel, the culture, the climate and the extreme difficulty of trying to integrate alternative transportation into a rapidly growing global metropolis. We knew that this was a very demanding client with the capability to make our visions for their city happen. It was a high wire act of epic proportions.

Our client, the Roads and Transportation Authority of Dubai (RTA) was very clear about its intentions to create a world-class destination city. They knew that Paris had implemented a major bikeshare system, that Stockholm had set a goal of zero pedestrian fatalities, and that Sydney had hosted the green Olympics. Dubai was also very clear about its vision of the future as the air travel hub for a 24-hour connected planet. If you look at a map of the Middle East, the next modern western-style city is a long way from Dubai. Singapore, Western Europe and Cape Town are all more than a thousand miles away. The populations of India, Africa and the Middle East have very few options in terms of places that provide safe, open, modern destinations. Dubai wants to be that destination.

I told our staff many times that this would be a very challenging project. The staff at RTA and other agencies in the Emirates were highly educated, sophisticated and knowledgeable. Many of the people we were working with had Ph.D's from Oxford, MIT and other top schools. The pace of growth was exponential when compared to the United States, and probably unmatched in any part of the world other than China. Dubai's development pattern was a cross between Shanghai and Las Vegas, with multilane highways in the place of urban streets. It was a dangerous place to be a pedestrian or bicyclist, and more people were being killed in traffic on the streets of Dubai than in New York each year.

We entered into this project with our eyes open, knowing that it was a major challenge for us, our client and the Emirates. It was difficult to balance the need to be both visionary and practical at the same time. We had to solve practical problems, such as creating safe pedestrian access to bus stops along busy roads (and yes, the bus shelters in Dubai are air conditioned). We also had to create a vision of these changes within the framework of a global city (we proposed some big ideas, including a glass pedestrian tunnel under the harbor, and a climate controlled bicycle sports park, complete with indoor mountain biking). We were asked to integrate safe access to the Dubai Metro System, which was under construction at the same time that we were planning and designing the solutions for pedestrians and bicyclists.

We had worked on big city projects, but Dubai took us to a new level. During the project, I flew to our office in Portland, set up Google Earth on a projector for the project team in our conference room, and had Brett call us on Skype every morning for a week. He would tell us what maps and graphics he needed, which streets we had to develop concepts for, what international research he needed done. At the end of his evening, our morning would start, and we'd get to work and be ready to send him what he needed for the next day in Dubai. For one call, we had team members on the line from Amsterdam, in our Portland office and Brett in Dubai – all collaborating on this unique project. Welcome to the modern world.

One moment in the project summarized the experience of working in Dubai. Brett had been asked to do a high-level presentation to key officials at RTA. Several of us helped to develop a powerpoint file, and I provided some slides on policy-level actions, including Complete Streets. Brett was invited to RTA's headquarters and asked to sit in a waiting area until the executives were ready for him. He waited for a couple of hours, knowing that the scheduled time for his presentation had already passed, and that he was only supposed to be on the agenda for ten minutes.

When Brett finally got into the room, the chief executive was on his mobile phone, having a heated discussion in Arabic. Minutes went by, and finally he said to Brett, "go ahead, you have 5 minutes." Brett, seeing his time already had been cut in half, started in on the presentation. After a couple of minutes, the executive took another call on his mobile, again in Arabic. When he finished, he said 'thank you' to Brett and told him the presentation was over. Brett quickly said, "One more slide" and clicked on the slide entitled "Complete Streets." The executive said, "OK – tell me what this means," and Brett gave a quick overview on the concept of integrating all modes of travel into all highway and transportation projects. The executive said,

"Excellent," and then took out his phone, spoke again in Arabic, and then said in English, "Complete Streets – make this our new policy for Dubai." The next day, the policy was put into effect by the RTA.

It is incredible to see leadership turn ideas into action so quickly. On my next trip to Dubai, I was shown how the Complete Streets policy was being put into practice. We were invited to a meeting with RTA and a major developer from Hong Kong who was designing a new series of island communities for 250,000 people. The designers had bookmarked a copy of our new Dubai Bicycle Master Plan, and showed us how the Plan had influenced the design for the new community. Every street, bridge, transit station, ferry dock and waterfront esplanade included high-quality facilities for bicyclists. The new development included more than 100 kilometers of new complete streets and greenways. Both the developer and RTA were proud of the ability to integrate new, state-of-the art third mode solutions into their work.

The global economic downturn of 2008 had a significant effect on major projects in the U.A.E. In addition to the work in Dubai, we had also taken on the bicycle and pedestrian master plans for Abu Dhabi, and had done a bike plan for Qatar. Much of our work was caught up in a shutdown of all work on transportation projects in the Emirates, and we had to deal with long delays in getting payments approved for the work we completed. This is part of the challenge of working in a global marketplace – especially as a small company working on overseas projects. At the same time, these challenging projects have led to real results – data are showing improved traffic safety and mobility in the

U.A.E., and we were challenged to push our work to new levels on these projects.

It should not be assumed that the U.A.E. projects were easy, or that they will be fully implemented. A particularly challenging issue in Dubai is the disparity between the wealthy Emirati and the larger population of laborers from Iran, India, Pakistan, and other nations who are building and maintaining the desert oasis city. Both rich and poor suffer from the overdependence on fossil fuels. A disproportionate percentage of Emirati men are experiencing the classic symptoms of the global inactivity pandemic, with high levels of diabetes becoming a major health issue. Increasing walking and bicycling can be part of the solution, and we proposed shaded, spray-misted esplanades along Dubai's waterfront areas to encourage this activity. An equally disproportionate percentage of the labor population is being killed as pedestrians and bicyclists in traffic collisions. Many of the laborers live in worker camp housing and need to walk, bicycle or take transit to work. Providing safe crossings of major roadways, access to transit and bikeways will help improve these conditions.

To better understand the reality of transportation inequity in the U.A.E., I took a bus ride to the Mall of the Emirates during one of my visits to Dubai. This required travelling on the local bus, not on the high quality regional bus system or the world-class new Dubai Metro System. The Metro has Silver and Gold class seating to provide accommodations for women, families and elite travelers. On the local bus, the route goes through a corridor of labor housing camps, many of which do not have paved streets. The buildings are pre-fabricated concrete walkups. The camps are within view of the glittering skyscrapers of Sheik Zayed Road. The world's tallest building rises in the distance.

I was the only white person on the local bus. It was crowded with laborers, many of them wearing their required blue coverall uniforms. When we got near the Mall of the Emirates, I had to get off the bus at the nearest point to the Mall – more than half a mile away and across an eight-lane divided highway with no pedestrian crossings. I waited for a few passengers to start running across the highway in between gaps in traffic, and then followed at full speed in the desert heat. I barely made it to the median in the middle of the road, waited, and then completed my sprint to the other side. I got to the curb in a suburban strip mall, with sand where the sidewalks should have been. I could see the Mall in the distance like a desert mirage on steroids. The road I was on looked like the back streets of Las Vegas.

I walked through the strip mall parking lots and found myself at the loading dock ramps and parking lot entrance for the Mall of the Emirates. I had to sprint across the high-speed ramps in the blinding heat, through heavy traffic and into the shade of the parking garage. I was pouring sweat from a combination of the desert afternoon temperature and the fear of taking my life in my hands just to get across the road. Inside the garage, it looked like a showroom for luxury vehicles, with Porches, BMW's, Mercedes and hordes of deluxe SUV's parked several floors high. The mall entrance was like walking into an air conditioned daydream, and in seconds I was in a world that was as far from the bus I'd travelled on as you could possibly imagine.

Unlike the people I'd shared the bus ride with, I was able to enjoy the glory of the Mall of the Emirates. I had lunch at one of the hundreds of restaurants, window-shopped at the endless, glittering high-end stores, and sat in the lobby of the opulent Kempinski Hotel. I then did the one thing that made the least possible sense on a blistering hot day in the Middle East – I went indoor skiing at the Mall of the Emirates. Ski Dubai is one of the most surreal experiences possible in this world. In the middle of the glitzy shopping mall, an indoor ski slope rises like a giant frosted cupcake, complete with a chairlift and a Swiss Chalet mid-station. I walked into the lobby, swiped my credit card, rented skis, boots, poles and overalls, took the escalator up to the chairlift, and within ten minutes I was on top of a small indoor mountain covered with man-made snow in the middle of the desert.

I rode up the lift with a snowboarding instructor from Nepal. He had moved from his home in the Himalaya like so many other expats in Dubai – in search of a job. He laughed at the fact that he came from a place 10,000 feet above sea level to teach snow sports in a shopping mall. I have to admit, I enjoyed skiing indoors and took as many runs as I could on my two hour ticket. It was fun to watch other skiers, many of whom clearly did not live in places with snow. I watched a young couple taking photos of each other, posing for images that could only happen in Dubai, only in our modern world, only in a place where issues of energy, environment, climate change and sustainability don't seem to matter – at least for a few moments, on an indoor ski slope in the desert.

After I came to my senses, I returned back down the escalator to the lobby at the same time as the young photogenic couple.

As I took off my ski boots, I was amazed to see that they were dressed in formal wear under their Ski Dubai jumpsuits – she was in a bright yellow ball gown, he was in a stylish suit and tie. I walked out, strolled through the mall, and decided to go out and see more of the tourist side of Dubai. I took a taxi to the famous Burj al Arab Hotel on Jumiera Beach. The driver let me off at a public beach with a view of the 7-star resort hotel, and in the same hour that I'd been skiing indoors, I was walking on the beach at sunset. Within a few minutes, I noticed a young couple posing for glamorous photos in the sand – and realized that it was the same yellow dress from Ski Dubai. I offered to take some photos for them, and they said that they'd just gotten married in Dubai, because where else in the world could you have a wedding, go skiing and walk on the beach all in the same afternoon?

It's impossible to grasp what this experience means. Clearly, Dubai is a fantasy view of the future. The indoor skiing and 7-star beach experience is not part of the same world that has migrant workers living in camps, where climate change is a real threat, where energy is not unlimited. To bring these issues back down to earth, we at least need to recognize the connection between the first part of my day spent taking public transportation and surviving the streets of Dubai as a pedestrian, and the relationship to the broader issues of economics, environment and energy. At a fundamental level, the design of the built environment cannot continue to be based on a single mode of transportation (the automobile) or even on two modes of transportation (automobiles and public transit). In order to create a safe, healthy, sustainable public realm, we need these options plus the third mode solutions of walking and bicycling.

As I had seen on my trip to the Mall, Dubai is, oddly enough, similar to Las Vegas. Both cities exist in a desert fantasy, and are currently built on their belief in cheap air travel, unlimited fossil fuel and drinking water. In spite of the sun and wind, there are very few solar collectors or wind generators in view. The Las Vegas Strip and Dubai's Sheik Zayed Road are both megastreets, with towering buildings along a multilane road-way designed beyond the human scale. In both cases, high numbers of pedestrian fatalities and injuries are a significant issue. Both streets are rapidly evolving, and in fact, investors from the UAE have made a significant real estate investment in Las Vegas.

Working in Dubai connected to a project I had been involved with earlier in my career. In 1996, I was part of a team led by Dan Burden of Walkable Communities, Inc. to redesign the Las Vegas Strip from a pedestrian's perspective. This was an extraordinary project at the time. The opportunity to work on the pedestrian problems of the Las Vegas Strip was a dream-come-true. The project was funded by the National Highway Traffic Safety Administration (NHTSA), and when Dan called me I jumped at the chance to be part of it.

We arrived in Las Vegas on a Monday morning, and were told we'd have one week to produce an action plan. There would be a presentation to the Mayor on Friday morning. Our task seemed impossible. The project included three study areas, and I was asked, along with John Moffat of Seattle, to lead the team making recommendations for the Strip. We were assigned a group of a dozen volunteers, and we met for the first time that day. We quickly realized that we had an eclectic and talented group, including John (a former vice squad officer who became the head of the Washington State Governor's Traffic Safety Committee) and Rick Romer of Clark County Public Works (a great traffic engineer who became an international leader of the Institute of Transportation Engineers), along with a casino vice president, local consultants and other interested parties.

Within the first couple of hours, John and I figured out that we had enough talent in our volunteer group to solve the technical aspects of the problem. Rick Romer had developed a formula that could calculate the volumes of pedestrians at intersections. Local consultants were already looking into providing tree lined medians along the Strip. The casino officials were well aware of the high numbers of pedestrian fatalities and injuries. What seemed to be missing was a bigger vision of what the Strip could be – and how to overcome its history as an automobile-dominated suburban highway in the midst of a rapidly developing city.

John and I got our team working on the basics of pedestrian safety solutions, and then moved into trying to figure out how to get the project to connect with elected officials, businesses and local leadership. We quickly found a graphic artist and started working on a series of illustrations. He started drawing backgrounds from photographs we had taken (this was in the era before digital cameras and Photoshop, so we knew this was going to take some time) while we convened a focus group that evening at a German beer garden. We asked around the table: what are the iconic images that define Las Vegas? How can we make those images part of the design of the Strip? In less than an hour we had dozens of ideas ranging from slot machine levers to activate pedestrian crossing signals, medians inlaid with coins, runway lights to define crosswalks, and crossing guards dressed in the costumes of the adjacent casinos.

When we reconvened the next day and shared these ideas with the larger team, they knew that we were onto something. Suddenly, a simple safety project had evolved into a much bigger vision of what a street could be. People who had been trying to provide basic pedestrian improvements on the Strip realized that what local leaders really cared about was the buzz, the excitement, the glamour of Las Vegas. They could easily imagine showgirls (and guys) stopping traffic as crossing guards, cafés on palm tree-lined sidewalks, and the extension of the adjacent casino designs right out into the street. We put together a presentation that showcased these ideas, with the traffic safety features hidden behind a Vegas façade. The mayor and community leaders loved the ideas. I can't say that all of them were implemented (the crossing guards were more than the NHTSA people would accept) but we did get people to realize that if Las Vegas wanted the Strip to be a great street, then they needed to make sure it worked for pedestrians, bicyclists and all other 'third mode' forms of mobility.

Like Las Vegas, Dubai's new infrastructure programs are trying to make this change happen. The early build-out of a highway-based city is now transitioning to a high quality transit system including the Dubai Metro and an excellent bus network. The third mode is being implemented as the pedestrian and bicycle master plans are being put into practice. It is now possible to imagine the motorist-oriented Sheik Zayed Road evolving into a complete street as Sheik Zayed Boulevard, with the new rail transit line, fewer lanes of motor vehicles, tree-lined medians and safe spaces for people walking and bicycling. A major lesson from both Dubai and Las Vegas is that it would be easier to create Complete Streets before new developments get built in the first place. The new Dubai policy is a major step in this direction. Clearly, if the United Arab Emirates can develop third mode solutions for walking and bicycling, then any community in the world can do it, too. If the challenges of a hot, desert climate and the cultural barriers of the Middle East are not a barrier to creating the third mode in Dubai, then anything is possible.

# 10. NW ARKANSAS

## A New Way of Thinking

Getting the U.S. and the rest of the world to believe in green infrastructure based on the third mode is little like trying to steer an aircraft carrier with a canoe paddle. For so many years, Americans have believed that what we need is more technology, more energy, more of everything to move forward. A classic example of the inability to see the green future is the Erie Canal Trail in upstate New York. The Erie Canal once transformed our nation by linking the Great Lakes and the Hudson River. Eventually, the canal was replaced by railroads, and the railroads were replaced by the interstate highway system. The original canal was built in less than a decade in the early 1800s using mostly manual labor. It has taken our generation more than 20 years to develop a trail across the canal – and that project is only partially complete.

If New York State's leaders could understand some basics about time and distance, they would be investing heavily in the Erie Canal and making the trail a top priority. The 325 mile canal trail connects the cities of Albany, Troy, Schenectady, Utica, Rome, Syracuse, Rochester, Buffalo, and Niagara Falls, along with dozens of small communities along the way. When the original Canal was in operation, freight moved at about eight miles an hour across the state, so each city was a day's travel apart. When the railroads first started, there was a huge outcry that their new speed – fifteen miles an hour – would destroy local communities because travel was too fast and required fewer stops along the way. Today's interstate highways move people and goods across the state at 65 miles per hour, and it is now possible to go from Buffalo to Albany in five hours, without stopping in any of the towns along the way.

For a bicyclist going across New York State, the canal trail would allow travel at a speed of between ten and fifteen miles per hour - faster than the old canal boats, and slower than today's highway. This would once again allow for travel between cities that are one day apart from each other, with towns in between for mid-day breaks. From an economic development perspective, this is the ideal combination – people who are hungry, thirsty and tired and don't have a car to take them to the next town. Unfortunately, most of the State's investment along the canal corridor has been to build new harbors and facilities for boats, to reconstruct bridges and highway projects on the interstate system, and to continue pursuing high-speed rail across the state. Meanwhile, the canal trail remains incomplete, waiting for a day when leaders realize the power of the third mode as a sustainable economic engine.

As public sector funding for non-motorized mobility continues to be a challenge at the local, state and federal levels, a new model is emerging with corporate and philanthropic leadership taking on a major role in sustainable development. In Detroit, the Community Foundation of Southeast Michigan has created a $100 million dollar urban greenways program with funding from philanthropic sources used to match federal funding. In the Charlotte, NC region, the Carolina Thread Trail system is following a similar model. Denver's award winning urban trails system has included major private sector contributions, including the REI flagship store at Confluence Park on the Platte River. Pittsburgh, Minneapolis and San Francisco have built new sports stadiums along their urban greenways. The innovation and creativity of private businesses, philanthropy and the non-profit "third sector" are well positioned to help create 'trail oriented development' in ways that expand sustainable mobility in new directions.

In the spring of 2010, I received one of those rare messages that leads to major changes. The Walton Family Foundation in Bentonville, Arkansas, wanted to talk about greenways. The Foundation wanted to know how they could serve as a catalyst to create a sustainable mobility system for their home region in Northwest Arkansas. They wanted to bring together a team of leaders to develop a new vision for their community's future. What made this request so extraordinary was that it came from the home of Wal-Mart, a corporation often perceived as a major cause of suburban sprawl. Even more amazing was that the Walton Family Foundation wanted to change this perception, and they were willing to start with their own home region.

The request from the Foundation was forwarded to me through Andy Clarke of the League of American Bicyclists. Andy had tried to get us to meet with some leaders in Bentonville the previous year, and he indicated that this could be something big. I returned the call from the Foundation within minutes. In that initial conversation, it was clear that this was going to be a very rare opportunity. As luck would have it, I was with my friend and national greenways expert Bob Searns in Denver that day, and we were able to quickly assemble a "Green Team" of leaders in the trails movement. Bob and Bill Neuman of Denver, Chuck Flink from North Carolina, fundraising specialist Tom Woiwode from Detroit, and the local firm CEI Engineering in Bentonville all agreed to collaborate on this new adventure. The group became known as the NW Arkansas Green Team.

Within a week we developed a proposal to the Foundation to host an initial 'listening session' to gather information about greenways in Northwest Arkansas. At that point, we knew that there was significant potential in the region, but we did not know how to best help the Foundation and its partners capitalize on the opportunity. As a team, we discussed providing the Foundation with a traditional regional master plan proposal, but instead agreed to submit a more open approach that could work as either a single workshop or lead into something larger. The Foundation liked our approach and invited the Green Team to set up a one week workshop with representatives of the six cities in their home region.

Within a month after our initial contact, we were ready to start. What we didn't realize was that this was about to become more than just a simple greenways plan - we were on our way towards a new model for how green infrastructure can shape sustainable development. At the first NW Arkansas Greenways workshop, it was clear that this was a region that was ready to think in the third mode. The Mayors of each city literally came to the table, rolled up their sleeves along with their staff, and worked as part of the team. Representatives from Bentonville, Rogers, Springdale, Lowell, Johnson, and Fayetteville worked collaboratively. Catalyst projects funded by the Walton Foundation were already in progress. Planners, landscape architects, engineers and community leaders all were willing to work together at a regional scale.

Within the first day, we had begun to map out a system that could potentially connect all six communities together. We spent time in the field, looked at potential corridors, and listened to developers, businesses and elected officials describe their visions for the future. The more the Green Team talked with community leaders, the more we all realized that there was no limit to what was possible for the region. As our team discussed the wide range of possible actions, we realized that a bold, visionary project was possible. By the end of the first week, we could begin to see the potential for a project that could catalyze the region: a new 40 mile Greenway linking all six cities in Northwest Arkansas.

The first workshop in NW Arkansas was so successful that we were invited back a few months later. The second session's purpose was to turn the regional "spine" greenway into a real project. As always, we showed up prepared with maps and data in hand, a detailed game plan and an outline of the documents we needed to create. During those sessions, I asked about naming the trail after the University of Arkansas icon – and the "Razorback" Greenway emerged as the name of the project. Working with local leaders, we mapped out each existing section of trail along the corridor, planned sections that were in the pipeline, and potential connections between these sections.

Once the communities could see the vision of a connected regional project, it was relatively easy to document the details of the alignment, potential costs and key challenges to implementation. The bigger challenge appeared to be how to create an organizational structure for implementing the project, and identifying potential sources of funding. The Green Team's fundraising and development group proposed a range of organizational structures, including setting up a new 'friends of the trail' non-profit, working within an existing regional agency such as the Northwest Arkansas Regional Planning Commission (NWARPC), and expanding the Walton Foundation's staff. We left these options flexible, knowing that the key to the organizational model would be the fundraising process.

The Walton Family Foundation had already invested in building several sections of new local pathways and trails, and it was clear that the regional project was the ideal way to capitalize on those projects. The Green Team worked with local partners to develop a set of high-quality design guidelines, a framework for a regional greenway management program, and a package of maps and graphics that could be used to pursue new funding opportunities. By the end of the second workshop, the NW Arkansas vision had emerged into a unique public – private – nonprofit partnership with the vision to create a 40 mile, $30 million dollar regional greenway corridor. The project will connect 6 cities, 23 schools, 3 hospitals, major corporations and an entire region – all based on the simple, third mode idea of being able to walk, bike and enjoy community trails.

The Razorback Greenway is a powerful new vision for Northwest Arkansas, and for other places. In many ways, the existing built environment in the region resembles most of the typical modern American landscape. Rapidly growing suburban corridors are replacing a landscape of farms and fields. This growth has been led by major corporations including Wal-Mart, Tyson Foods, and J.B. Hunt Transportation. Today, the defining public infrastructure investment in the region has been in roads and highways. Interstate 540 is now called the "Main Street" of Northwest Arkansas. The automobile is the primary form of mobility, and formerly rural local roads are now clogged suburban arteries. The former downtowns have had to compete with new malls and office parks. Traffic congestion, air pollution, public health and a loss of the region's quality of life are key issues. What is different about Northwest Arkansas is that local leaders are aware of these issues and are actively doing something about it.

Once we started discussing the idea of implementing the regional Razorback Greenway with the Foundation, it was clear that we had found the way forward into new territory. Everyone agreed that the concept was about more than a regional bike trail – it was an opportunity to literally change the way the region lived, worked and played. We were a little surprised at how quickly the Foundation said to run with the idea, and were amazed at how quickly all of the local leaders and communities reached consensus. Maybe we were initially cautious because we've all spent so many years dealing with opposition, grudgingly gaining acceptance of innovation, and overcoming challenges to similar projects. In Northwest Arkansas' case, they went from initial meeting to total support faster than any community I've seen.

To illustrate the extraordinary level of what's happening in NW Arkansas, it's worth looking at the redevelopment of downtown Bentonville. If your image of Wal-Mart is a faceless corporate giant destroying local communities with suburban sprawl, it's surprising to see what is happening in their hometown. The downtown square in Bentonville is the site of Sam Walton's original store. The square has been restored with a central fountain, the original store is now a museum of the company's history, the historic County courthouse frames the square, and a locally owned bike shop and café face the fountain. One of the owners of the bike shop is a young Wal-Mart executive.

One block away from the Bentonville town square, the new $28 million dollar, "21C" Hotel is being developed – the second location for the nation's premier art gallery hotel. The next block is a new water park and skating rink. Across from the water park is the trailhead of the new Bentonville Greenway - the gateway to hundreds of acres of recently donated open space that is full of brand new, world class single track mountain bike trails. The new open space lands are home to the new Crystal Bridges Museum of American Art, designed by architect Moshe Sadfie and funded by the Walton Family Foundation. The museum includes two bridges spanning a creek to create a human-made lake, and an art collection that rivals the Smithsonian. The greenway system connects the museum directly to downtown and adjacent neighborhoods.

Just below the new museum are the new Slaughter Pens Mountain Bike Park and miles of incredible single track trails. The trails, museum and public lands are projects led by members of the Walton Family. People of all ages and abilities are out on the trails. All of this is in the middle of the city of Bentonville, a short walk or bike ride from Wal-Mart headquarters, and created through innovative philanthropy. There are very few small cities in the U.S. that can match this investment in quality of life, and it is all based on a green infrastructure solution. Bentonville is the prototype "first mile" for the entire Razorback Greenway. The Greenway will, in turn, be the catalyst for connecting green infrastructure systems in all six cities in Northwest Arkansas, and the system will then connect the region's major worksites, hospitals, schools and destinations.

I have asked people at the Walton Family Foundation and at Wal-Mart Corporation about the perceived disconnect between the company's suburban sprawl image and the extraordinary level of support for these new projects in their home region. The consistent response is that a growing group within their leadership is aware that the company is currently known for its big-box suburban stores and must change as society changes in the future. They know that if they don't change and adapt, they will cease to be competitive. They see becoming a leader in green infrastructure as part of that process. They know that building a bicycle-friendly corporate headquarters is essential for employee health, that creating a high quality of life is part of their region's ability to attract and retain business. They are leading the effort in their home region to prove this point. It will be very interesting to see if this initiative can be carried over into other Wal-Mart locations and into the home regions of their suppliers and customers.

With the vision of the 'first mile' on the ground in Bentonville and the concept of the Razorback Greenway as a catalyst, we continued to be inspired by the potential in NW Arkansas. After the initial Master Plan process, the Foundation asked the Green Team to develop a detailed implementation strategy. The task at hand wasn't 'why should we do this?' – it was 'how quickly can we get it done.' That feeling has been building in the U.S. for the past decade as communities begin to understand the relationship between quality of life, green infrastructure and economic development. The difference in this project was the rare combination of a good idea, great leadership and the resources to make it happen.

In a way, working with the Walton Family Foundation is similar to working with the Rockefellers, The Gates Foundation or the Medici during the Italian Renaissance– they all have had the ability to use their wealth and resources to change the future. In our discussions with the Walton Family Foundation, we realized that they were already providing a significant amount of funding for local greenway projects such as the Bentonville trails. The Foundation had been providing funding for local projects on a 1 to 1 matching basis. This greatly exceeded the funding ratio required for federally funded projects, which generally required communities to provide only a 20% match. We knew that if they could leverage their resources as matching funds for federal funding, there would be significant potential to expand the NW Arkansas regional trails program.

It is often said that you make your own luck. Shortly after we completed the Razorback Greenway Master Plan, we had a fortunate coincidence when the USDOT announced a new transportation funding program called TIGER II. TIGER was an acronym for Transportation Investments Generating Economic

Recovery. The requirements for TIGER II included sustainability, economic development, livability, and the support of public private partnerships. This was a major shift in focus for the U.S. stimulus funding programs provided during the economic recovery programs of the Obama administration. Most of the early stimulus funds had gone to "shovel ready" projects that consisted of mainly rebuilding existing highways and roads. In my opinion, the previous stimulus funds had done nothing more than rebuild the automobile- oriented infrastructure of the 1980s. We had said from the beginning of the Razorback Greenway project that it was a potential model for a new approach to green infrastructure, and now we had our chance to prove that point.

The Walton Family Foundation asked our team to write the TIGER II grant application. The NWARPC agreed to be the official applicant. The Foundation agreed to commit up to $15 million dollars in matching funds, and since the TIGER II program did not have a specified match amount, we agreed that the application could request approximately $20-25 million dollars in federal funding. We knew we had the right project – the challenge was putting together a winning application against a national competition for limited funding. When I mentioned that a critical element would be generating letters of support from throughout the region, the Foundation agreed to host a meeting of key leaders and asked me to help facilitate.

We met for lunch at a NW Arkansas country club, and the room was filled with all the right people – the bankers, state agencies, corporations, and elected officials who could make this project happen. When they asked me 'what do you need?"

I fully realized just how extraordinary this project was. I said we needed written letters of support from everyone at the table, from the Governor's office to the Chamber of Commerce, and the region's Congressional delegation. The group around the table said 'done' and moved on to lunch. By the time we finished the meeting, we had commitments that resulted in more than 40 letters of support from all the key leaders in the region. The Northwest Arkansas Council, a local business leadership organization, agreed to arrange visits to DC if needed, the Arkansas Highway and Transportation Department agreed to help with the application paperwork, and the University of Arkansas agreed to allow the project to be named the Razorback Greenway.

This kind of total regional support is rare for greenways in the U.S. To have a project involving six cities go from concept to master plan to implementation with the full support of its regional leadership in less than one year is the way these projects should be – but not the way they usually are. With this rare level of support, writing the TIGER II grant application was easy. The application was limited to 25 pages and could only be submitted electronically. I kept telling our team that what they were producing was worth $1 million per page. Once the application was submitted by NWARPC, along with all the letters of support, the NW Arkansas leadership provided follow-up phone calls, handwritten personal notes and office visits to key supporters in Washington DC.

We did not know how long the review process would take at USDOT, but I kept saying that since it was a federal program, chances were that the announcements would be connected to the upcoming election season. On Oct 20, 2010 the USDOT announced that the Razorback Greenway had been awarded $15 million in Tiger II funding. Our project was one of only two greenway projects (the other was in San Francisco) selected from almost 700 applications. Of the billions of dollars in application requests competing for the $600 million available, our project was awarded 2.5% of the national total. This would not have happened without the incredible level of support generated by the NW Arkansas region. It seemed at this point that we had finally achieved a nearly perfect project – an efficient, effective planning process that would lead quickly to implementation of a major regional greenway system.

Unfortunately, as it turns out, we were still in the United States of the early 21st century. The NW Arkansas region's level of support would be critical in overcoming a surprising series of new obstacles. Just when we thought the project would move full speed ahead, national politics got in the way. In the elections that followed the TIGER II funding announcement, one of the mayors from a city along the greenway was elected to the US Congress. Initially, this seemed like a great asset, since all of the mayors had been personally involved in the planning process, and they all had provided letters of support for the TIGER II application.

However, the new congressman was a member of the Republican Party's new Tea Party movement to reduce the size of government. When he got to Washington, his first piece of legislation was House of Representatives Bill Number HR1 of 2011, which proposed to eliminate the entire TIGER II funding program. In spite of the objections of voters at home and community leaders in NW Arkansas, the politics of the season trumped any form of logic. The former mayor voted, as a new member of the United States Congress, to eliminate the funding for a $30 million dollar project in his own community, in order to stick with his political party's new ideology. You can't make this stuff up. What a country we live in.

To make matters even stranger, the vote of this Congressman earned him the respect of his peers – and did not even lead to the loss of federal funding. Fortunately, the U.S. legislative process is a three-part system, and HR1 required approval in both the Senate and by the President in order to become law. Strategically, the supporters of the Razorback Greenway went to their Senators to prevent the TIGER II funding from being eliminated. The Senators delayed the cuts recommended by HR1, and the project was extended long enough for the federal funding to be obligated for the project. In what amounted to a "hero vote," both the Senators and the Congressman were able to save face, and the project continued to move forward. In all of this debate, little consideration was given to the fact that it was philanthropy that was the driving force for the project – a fact that should have overridden the agony of two party politics.

To move forward, the Razorback Greenway project still had to survive other bureaucratic obstacles. For one thing, the TIGER II grant award was for less than the amount the region had applied for. Fortunately, the Green Team had anticipated this possible outcome in the grant application and had written in elements of the trail that could be funded separately, such as trailheads, public art, benches and other amenities. We also realized that two of the six communities (Fayetteville and Bentonville) had resources available to complete their sections without federal funding, so we were able to focus the TIGER II resources in the communities that needed the money the most. As a result, the TIGER II funded project was defined as the central section of the Razorback Greenway in the communities of Rogers, Springdale and Johnson. The overall project will still be a 40 mile regional spine, but this flexible approach allowed the project to move forward.

Another challenging hurdle was that a key part of the federal aid funding process is the National Environmental Policy Act (NEPA) review process. In order to proceed, even a 'green' infrastructure project has to receive, at a minimum, a Categorical Exclusion (CE) from the Federal Highway Administration stating that there are no significant environmental issues. Typically, the environmental review process is done as part of the preliminary design of a project. Since the NWARPC had served as the applicant for the federal funding, the Walton Family Foundation had chosen to channel their financial support for project design services through the regional planning agency. Knowing that the TIGER II program had a strict 24 month schedule for getting through the design process, the Green Team had submitted a detailed scope for project design services to the Foundation as soon as the funding was announced.

However, the Foundation and NWARPC decided that instead of directly awarding the design contract, it made sense to go through an open public request for proposals. Even though it would take time and cause a possible delay, this would ensure that all parties had gone through the appropriate due diligence for a project of this scale. We agreed with this approach, even though it could mean that other firms would compete for the work, and valuable time was going by. As it turned out, 17 firms submitted proposals. After reviewing the submittals, the Green Team was awarded a first-phase contract to conduct field work and complete the NEPA CE process.

There was considerable discussion about the scope and scale of the CE documentation. In our team's previous national experience, the CE documents were detailed reports with extensive maps and exhibits that certified the project's lack of environmental impact. In discussions with the state and FHWA, the staff at NWARPC believed that the CE could be streamlined and approved in a five page document at a single meeting. This would be the first time a project had been handled this way. A meeting was set up in Little Rock for the first week of April. Since this was the same week that the TIGER II funding had been extended to by Congress, it was critical that the CE get approved in time to obligate the federal funding.

The first step towards getting the CE approved was 'ground truthing' the corridor – literally walking the entire project and documenting environmental issues. At the master plan level, we had used aerial photos and local knowledge to identify the potential route. To get the project CE approved, this critical next step was required to fully document the physical challenges and opportunities along the corridor. The Green Team, led by our Project Manager Chuck Flink, assembled in NW Arkansas in March 2011 and in one week walked the entire route, mapped it using GPS units, took extensive photographs, and sketched plans and cross sections. Each day was spent walking a section, and each evening was spent drawing and documenting the field conditions. By the end of the week, it was clear that not only did the project have no negative environmental impacts, but that it would create new areas for habitat conservation, historical interpretation, and improved human health.

In a rare moment of coordinated public, private and no-profit efforts, the CE environmental review process for the Razorback Greenway was completed within a month of the field review. A team approach was used to get state, federal and regional agencies literally on the same page – and all the interested parties came together at the meeting in Little Rock for a simultaneous review of the project. The state and federal agencies approved the Categorical Exclusion for the project, which allowed the USDOT to formally obligate the TIGER II funding. The CE is not the same as giving the project a "positive" approval for its environmental benefits, but it was a major step forward. Multiple permits are still required from the Army Corps of Engineers, the State Historic Preservation Office and local agencies. Someday, all of these processes will be streamlined for green infrastructure projects. The Razorback Greenway showed that such a process is possible, but full implementation of that concept will have to wait for another day.

The Razorback Greenway still has a long way to go, but it is well on its way to implementation faster than the generation of projects that preceded it in other regions. The Green Team's design group, led by Chuck Flink, has successfully produced the detailed design work in partnership with a group of engineering firms based in Northwest Arkansas. The NWARPC has taken on management of the federal aid process, and the Walton Family Foundation has been able to stay quietly in the background, allowing all of the local communities to share the limelight. In July of 2011, USDOT Secretary Ray LaHood visited the region for a ceremony highlighting the Razorback Greenway, it was a significant moment, coming just a week after Republicans in the U.S. Congress had proposed new legislation to prevent federal transportation funding from being spent on bicycle, pedestrian and trail projects. Secretary LaHood was the only Republican in the Obama Administration, and he clearly believes in the power of the third mode.

Time will tell if the Razorback Greenway achieves its full potential. Even with the incredible level of support the project enjoys, it is clear that green infrastructure is still far from mainstream in the region and most of the U.S. What sets Northwest Arkansas apart at this point has been the region's unique ability to harness a powerful public, private and non-profit collaboration to take a visionary idea into reality. With leadership from philanthropy, this project is a potential model for how the private sector can lead the transformation of the built environment. By being open to new ideas and seeing the third mode as a real solution to complex issues, the Razorback Greenway can help prove that transportation, recreation and innovation are the keys to a sustainable future.

# *Now What?*

## CONCLUSION

## Toward a Green Society

To be honest, I'm not sure if these projects and stories are meaningful, or if they can be seen as symbolic of broader changes that are emerging in our society. I do know that from the current issues of climate change, the global obesity pandemic, the rise of nature deficit disorder, and other trends of the modern world, we are at a fork in the road. The world we live in can stay the same, go backwards, change by crisis, or be changed because we choose to create solutions to global issues. Combinations of these paths are possible. We may live in some version of Jorge Louis Borges' great short story "The Garden of the Forked Paths," where there are multiple possible alternatives. Sometimes life does imitate art.

While I have been writing this book, the U.S. Congress has been passing a new transportation bill called "MAP 21 – Moving Ahead for Progress in the 21st Century" that will reduce the amount of funding available for walking, bicycling and trails. This new bill might as well have been called "More Automobiles, Please." The legislation eliminated the Safe Routes to Schools program, and does not include a provision for Complete

Streets. What does it mean that, for the past 50 years, we have left the third mode solution of walking and bicycling out of our highways versus transit transportation debate? Does it really matter if we use new thinking to find real 10% solutions to major issues? From my point of view, an environmental review system that fails to recognize a "positive" project, a monoculture of engineering that ignores the definition of "traffic," and National Parks that allow themselves to become parking lots, are all symbolic of bigger issues. If the stories in this book are to be of any lasting value, it has to be about a larger perspective than the projects on these pages. When Lance Armstrong said, "It's not about the bike" he was describing a similar perspective.

If, in any of the examples I have described, the third mode had been the way people had been thinking at the beginning of the problem, bigger changes would have been possible. In each case, those solutions would have had ripple effects at even larger scales. Every individual who chooses to think in the third mode becomes a new voice in their organization, their business and their community. These leaders then become part of larger groups that have the ability to shape a larger vision of society. You may think that one person riding a bike to school is an insignificant change. I think it is significant. If that person helps a whole school make that change, that school in turn can change a whole community. As Margaret Mead said, "never doubt that a small group of concerned citizens can change the world. Indeed it's the only thing that ever has."

You never know if one person who changes their thinking could be the next Lance Armstrong. He grew up without a parent to chauffer him around all the time, and had to ride his bike several miles to swim practice every day. The miles on the bike, the hours in the pool and his competitive nature helped make him a champion triathlete and seven-time Tour de France winner. He then became a global ambassador for finding the cure for cancer. Every time I see a street become safer for bicyclists and pedestrians, I wonder how many kids – and adults – now have a chance to move around in a new way, to see the world under their own power, and to maybe, just maybe – start to change the world.

I am a realistic optimist. There continue to be opportunities to make change happen if we recognize the kind of third mode thinking that will help us see the solutions. As I said before, I don't see the third mode as a 100% solution to all of the world's problems. At the same time, I do see the potential for thinking beyond the two-dimensional, bi-modal mindset that we are currently stuck in. I'd like to hope that we can change society in a positive way through good planning, a better understanding of the challenges we face, and new ways of thinking. Unfortunately, a large segment of society keeps hoping that some new technology will solve all of our problems for us, that the problems don't exist, or that our problems will simply go away without us having to change.

If we keep thinking the same way, the transportation industry will remain focused on cars, without realizing that even if we all start driving hybrids, we will still have too many cars on our roads. The energy industry will remain focused on finding new sources of fossil fuels, including "hydrofracking" for natural gas and drilling new oil wells in fragile ecosystems. The healthcare industry will keep looking for that miracle drug to cure cancer, heart disease and diabetes so that our lifestyles can continue in the status quo. As the world's population grows and cities continue to expand, the third mode is an increasingly necessary solution. As China, India, and other developing nations grow their economies, the demand for a new way of thinking is becoming critical. We need real changes that can be put in place today, and that can make those 10% solutions a reality.

Third mode ideas can help communities, individuals and organizations see new kinds of solutions. I am always looking for the moments in our projects when a challenge can become a catalyst. This is often an opportunity to create fun, innovative, visionary solutions. For example, when we were working on a plan for a ski resort town in California, a busy arterial street was seen as a barrier by the community. We developed a photo-rendering that showed how an innovative "road diet" could turn that street into a ski slope by leaving the snow on it in winter, and adding a chairlift into a center median. In the Middle East, we illustrated a pedestrian tunnel under a busy harbor as a walk-through aquarium to highlight the local aquatic environment. In my own town, I proposed digging up a buried creek through the center of downtown as an alternative to building a cluster of parking garages in the same corridor. These are the kinds of ideas that come from using the third mode to look beyond the limits of a problem. Even if they don't happen in the short term, they can open people's eyes to new ways of seeing possible solutions that might otherwise have been overlooked.

I wish it wasn't true, but we often learn to see new ideas in times of crisis. Just a decade into the new Millennium, the U.S.

suffered through major tragedies on 9/11 and in the aftermath of Hurricane Katrina in New Orleans. Both disasters were microcosms of a future world where human and environmental factors force us to understand the basic conditions of how cities will work – or fail. There were many lessons learned in response to these tragedies, and sustainable mobility is only one of them. On both occasions we were forced to learn that our nation needs to become healthier, stronger, more self-sufficient and less dependent on emergency support. Since our society doesn't think of walking, bicycling and the self-reliance that comes with physical activity as major solutions to national issues, we keep relying on the most costly and energy intensive solutions to these problems.

In the worst of urban emergencies, we are forced to learn the obvious: when all else fails, people are pedestrians. Walking is the foundation of mobility - and a transportation system that misses this point is destined to fail. Clearly, not everyone could have walked away from Katrina or 9/11, but many people could have, and that would have helped make more of the limited available emergency resources available for the sick, the injured and those who had no other option. It shouldn't take another crisis to learn this, but we will have new crises. Hurricanes, snowstorms, earthquakes and other events will continue to challenge our ability to respond.

Two summers after 9/11, New York City was hit by a major power blackout. People who had been in the City during the terrorist attacks learned not to depend on motorized transport in another major emergency. Because so many people walked across the Brooklyn Bridge that night, they created what was reported to be the heaviest load the bridge had ever carried. People were aware that, during the blackout, driving a car or getting onto mass transit wouldn't work. They knew from experience that walking was their best option. As pedestrians, they were part of the solution, not part of the problem. Although walking may only help move people a few miles, it is an effective solution for large scale crowd movements in emergencies, and in everyday life.

I fully realize that these are extreme events, but they do bring out the kinds of solutions that can only be seen in times of crisis. When forced to do so, we can move large numbers of people using less energy, with greater physical activity, and without depending entirely on motorized technology. The challenge for this generation lies in choosing to make this change happen every day, before there is a crisis. We can invert the car-oriented transportation food pyramid and re-define mobility based on third-mode solutions. Since this happens spontaneously during times of crisis, it makes sense to capitalize on these solutions through intentional change the rest of the time. Walking and bicycling provide people with the ability to be independent, to control their mobility and to enjoy the freedom of movement. That is why these critical transportation options can become the foundation for mobility in our daily lives.

On September 11, 2001, the United States entered a new era. The story of America as an invincible, open, and fossil-fueled society has been changed forever. After the attacks, President Bush told our nation to go shopping and buy new cars. He did not call upon people to change. We saw poignant images of SUVs stuck in traffic jams, with American flags waving from their radio antennas. Was this the Star Spangled Banner of a new age? Are we prepared to fight to protect the sprawl of six lane arterial highways and placeless suburbia? Can we continue to afford the costs of our unsustainable use of fossil fuels? Or are we willing to meet the challenge of understanding the underlying basis for Middle Eastern terrorism: the fossil fuel economy. The irony of flag waving, gas guzzling, SUV drivers idling in suburban traffic should not be lost at this point in history. Until we realize the connection between our oil dependency and growing anti-American hatred, the causes of September 11 will continue to be unresolved.

These issues cannot be solved by military power. The disastrous wars in Iraq and Afghanistan have achieved little from a military or security perspective. We have lost another generation of soldiers, and it is still unclear why we are even fighting wars overseas when we have so many problems here at home. A friend of mine once said, "We don't need an energy policy in America – that's why we have the Marines." After Hurricane Katrina, President Bush had an historic opportunity to go to New Orleans and say, "we are bringing our troops home from around the world, and using all of our resources to rebuild this city and reverse the effects of climate change." He didn't to that, and as we continue fighting wars over oil, I don't feel any safer than I did a decade ago. I still have to take off my shoes every time I go through the airport. Our economy has been crushed by the mountain of debt racked up fighting foreign wars. We cannot afford to keep thinking that the only way to create change is by forcing it to happen.

In a more optimistic view, there are great events happening every day around the world to celebrate the connection between health, infrastructure and transportation. Every one of these events brings us closer to freedom, health and energy independence. From the historic Ramblas in Barcelona to the new pedestrian plazas on Broadway in Manhattan, we can see how great streets can be if we base their use on people first. Sunday Parkways and Ciclovias have turned urban roadways from Chicago's Lakeshore Drive to the boulevards of Mexico City into rolling celebrations of happy citizens. Every parade on the Main Street in a small town has the same potential effect –the temporary transformation of public space from priority space for motorists into priority space for people. The challenge is to find a way to make that transformation a more lasting part of everyday life in more communities.

We are at a cultural fork in the road. I still believe that we are capable of changing our consumptive lifestyle through conscious choice, but I don't know if we have enough time. As individuals, organizations, and as a society, we have the opportunity to choose our path into the future. If we don't take that opportunity, it isn't hard to imagine a day when our interstate highways have reverted back to footpaths because we've run out of oil, and a crisis economy forces us to become a nation of bicyclists and pedestrians because there is no other choice. That is the post-apocalyptic future that James Howard Kunstler envisions for us in his book, "The World Made by Hand." Our current fossil fuel based system has shown its Achilles heel in the past decade. The use of civilian aircraft as weapons, the inability to move people and goods in emergency situations, the anxiety produced by the growing costs for fuel to heat and cool our buildings, flooding and drought due to climate change, and the dependence on petroleum to grow and transport food – all of these issues are tied to the state of our infrastructure. The majority of the basic systems we depend on are simply not sustainable – and they are no longer absolutely defensible, either. As a nation of historic innovators, we must recognize the new issues brought about by current events: the need for energy independence, freedom of mobility and personal safety. Providing solutions to these issues requires us to live a more humble lifestyle, closer to the ideals of America's founders. Our society is wealthy because of the earth's natural resources. We must carry a deeper understanding of this fact with us into the future.

The time has come to accept this reality as the basis for a new Green Infrastructure. Green infrastructure is a sustainable system which supports an environment shared by people and nature. This is a simple, but potentially powerful definition. Instead of an adversarial relationship between humans and nature, green infrastructure benefits both. Unlike fossil fuel based systems, green systems are capable of true sustainability – the inputs required to set them in motion are used to continually supply the system. A green building is capable of generating its own light, heat, cooling and water from the same renewable resources as a photosynthetic plant. This is a concept which has been demonstrated through solar energy, wind power, water recycling and other green technologies.

A green mobility infrastructure is more complex. Unlike meeting the environmental needs of an individual building, transportation systems require people and goods to be moved across them. They typically consume energy rather than produce it. They function across state, local and international borders. Public, private and non-profit interests are involved in their funding, operation and maintenance. They are defining features that can shape the patterns of development for a neighborhood, a city or a metropolitan area. It is possible to imagine future cities where greenways are the main infrastructure corridors, lined with solar panels, wind generators, rain gardens, utility services and community gardens. The benefits of sustainable mobility can cut across the boundaries of multiple issues, providing simultaneous health, environmental and economic benefits. This is the beauty of the third mode.

What if we suddenly recognized the need to implement green mobility systems, and if these solutions were seen a part of a much broader social movement? What if the world's leaders seized the opportunity to use the third mode as a new vision for the future? We can dream, can't we? When President Obama was elected in November, 2008, I was one of the millions of people who believed that this kind of a new way forward was possible. Like so many others, I may have been naïve or idealistic about the potential for change. In fact, I still am. I do believe that the third mode is a new way of moving America and other nations, states, cities, organizations, businesses, people and communities forward. In the months leading up to President Obama's inauguration, I circulated the following message to a group of key people throughout the country. I had written what I imagined I would like to hear President Obama say in a speech to the nation. It never got used as a top level policy speech, but I still hope that it will someday. It may provide you with some food for thought, too - so here it is:

# The Green Society: America's Next 100 Days

America's new era begins today. We are living in an historic moment, with a unique opportunity to change ourselves, our nation and the world from crisis into opportunity, from fear to hope, from the past into the future. We are faced with unprecedented challenges in our economy, the environment, and in our ability to achieve America's vision of life, liberty and the pursuit of happiness. Now is the time for everyone in this nation to work together. What we have to do will not be easy. We need solutions that can happen today – we don't have the time to "drill baby drill" or build new power plants. We must work together, with leadership in the public, private, and non-profit sectors to encourage government, business and individuals to be a part of an historic change. As Bruce Springsteen has said during these difficult times, "we want our America back."

It is time for America to lead the world by finding solutions at home. The billions of dollars that we are spending each month on war must be redirected to get our nation back on its feet. In previous generations, President Franklin Roosevelt and President Dwight Eisenhower both turned to rebuilding America's infrastructure as a solution. Today, we must re-invest our resources in creating a Green Society: an America with a sustainable economy, energy independence, and a new vision of the American dream. As a first step, starting today, we will reduce our dependence on foreign oil by 10% within 100 days. This effort will be called "Ten Percent NOW." We will all share this responsibility by turning out extra lights, adjusting our thermostats, driving less, and making the personal choice to conserve.

Like Rosie the Riveter, "Yes we Can!" We can choose to walk, bike, carpool or take transit for one out of every ten trips we take. We can telecommute one day a week, change our work schedules, take the stairs instead of the elevator, turn off appliances that aren't in use, recycle cans, bottles and paper – these simple actions will save individuals money and reduce our energy consumption immediately. I will lead by personal example, reducing my carbon footprint by purchasing carbon credits for my energy usage. We will direct federal agencies to reduce their energy use by 10%. If we work together, this change will not require a tremendous sacrifice – if millions of individuals can each save 10%, together we can reach this goal as a nation.

But this is just a start – and in the next 100 days we will launch a range of new initiatives to make America a Green Society, including:

**One Billion Trees:** We will plant trees throughout this country – on our neighborhood streets, in our parks, at our schools, libraries and public buildings, along our highways, where we work, in our backyards and on our public lands. These trees will be a catalyst for our new Green Society. They will help remove greenhouse gasses from the atmosphere, add beauty and shade to our communities, and provide a cost effective, lasting symbol for the future. We will establish a Green Corps modeled after the CCC to plant trees and encourage conservation.

**Complete Main Streets:** We will build a new infrastructure to make our nation's Main Streets into "Complete Streets," that are safe for residents, visitors and the customers of local businesses. We will create new bike lanes, public squares, transit shelters, sidewalks and crosswalks – simple, cost effective improvements that can be implemented quickly to help reduce our nation's automobile dependence. We will bring wind, solar and other sustainable technologies into our homes, businesses and communities. We will establish a Green WPA to create green jobs building our new green infrastructure.

**National Greenways**: We will connect every region of this country with a National Greenways System –a new green version of our interstate highways. Forty years ago, President Lyndon Johnson signed the National Trails System Act, and now we will work together to build our nation's scenic and historic trails into a network from city to city and border to border, from sea to shining sea. This initiative will connect visionary projects such as the East Coast Greenway, the Mississippi River Trail, the American Discovery Trail, the West Coast Greenway and urban trail systems so we reach a goal of having a trail within 15 minutes of all Americans.

**President's Council on Physical Fitness:** We will encourage all Americans to meet basic levels of physical fitness to improve our lives and reduce our nation's health care costs. Obesity, heart disease and diabetes are at epidemic levels, and each of us can be part of the solution by eating well and getting more exercise. We will work with the "No Child Left Inside" initiative on outdoor programs for our youth to improve their physical, psychological and emotional health.

**Green Days:** We will encourage the celebration of Green Days – days where people celebrate living without depending on fossil fuels. We can enjoy 'car free days' and 'Sunday parkways' where roads are opened to people walking and bicycling – we've done this in Chicago and I know it can work in communities throughout the nation.

**Freedom Gardens:** We will create more community gardens and farmers' markets to include healthy food and a connection to the land in the lives of more Americans. This effort will be modeled after the Victory Gardens of the 1940' and will help bring more green into our neighborhoods.

**Safe Routes to Schools:** Our schools are struggling with the costs of energy and transportation, and we will work with the National Safe Routes to Schools Program to get more children walking and bicycling to school. This will improve health and safety in our communities and engage the next generation in the simple solutions that we can all be part of.

**Sustainable Buildings, National Parks and Public Lands:** We will make sure that solar, wind, geothermal and alternative transportation solutions are integrated throughout our nation's public places. Our lands and buildings will become models for saving energy, recycling and environmental stewardship. As our National Parks System moves towards the celebration of its centennial in 2016, we will create catalyst projects such as putting the solar panels back on the roof of the White House, completing the new Greenways system at Grand Canyon National Park, and making sure that our National Forests are sustainably managed.

This is just the beginning, but we have to start with a new beginning. Today, I chose to walk here to demonstrate that every choice we make is part of the solution. We all must walk in the footsteps of Ghandi and Martin Luther King, who inspired the world to create peaceful change. We must work together as individuals, organizations and as a nation. Every step we take matters, every gallon of foreign oil we save is an act of patriotism. Join me as we move forward into the future, as we add green to our great red, white and blue nation, as we create the Green Society.

Thank You

The President of the United States

I wrote this text on October 29, 2008 in Saratoga Springs, New York, as a citizen who hopes that someday the President of the United States, the Secretary General of the United Nations, CEO's of corporations, philanthropists, environmentalists, local leaders and individuals will use these words – in their own words - to create change. We all can dream, can't we?

Throughout this book I've asked you to think in a new way, to imagine how individuals, organizations, agencies, businesses and governments can make positive changes happen. There is no crystal ball to look into the future, but I hope that the stories on these pages will change your perspective. I hope that you will see that many of our biggest problems can't be solved by bi-modal thinking, and that the constant back and forth of us-versus-them decision making will only continue to create the motion of a pendulum. The third mode can help us move beyond the highways vs. transit paradox, two party politics and yes or no answers to complex issues. The stories I have told are just the beginning – it is now up to you to figure out how we can think differently. It is up to you to become part of the solution.

On a recent bike trip, I stopped at a country store in Vermont. It was evening, and there were huge thunderstorms ahead of me over Lake Champlain. I asked a man at the store if I should continue riding or wait at the store until the storms passed. He looked at me and said, "Both" and walked away. I stood there and laughed – what a great answer he had given me. It was not an either-or question. As it turned out, waiting a few minutes while the storms rolled across, and then biking down the road, led to seeing a spectacular sunset. From now on, if you are confronted with a problem that is defined by two opposites, stop, think, and imagine multiple solutions. If we want to move forward, we all need to think in the third mode.

Thank you for reading *The Third Mode*. We'd like to hear your comments and ideas. Please become part of The Third Mode community at *www.TheThirdMode.com*, or by friending *The Third Mode* on Facebook.